PETER BROOK

The Empty Space

A TOUCHSTONE BOOK
Published by Simon & Schuster

TOUCHSTONE
Rockefeller Center
1230 Avenue of the Americas
New York, NY 10020

First Touchstone Edition 1996

TOUCHSTONE and colophon are registered
trademarks of Simon & Schuster Inc.

Portions of this book were previously published in
The Atlantic Monthly

Manufactured in the United States of America

31   33   35   37   39   30   38   36   34   32

Library of Congress catalog card number 68–12531

ISBN 0–684–82957–6

FOR MY FATHER

CONTENTS

THE EMPTY SPACE

1

The Deadly Theatre

I CAN take any empty space and call it a bare stage. A man walks across this empty space whilst someone else is watching him, and this is all that is needed for an act of theatre to be engaged. Yet when we talk about theatre this is not quite what we mean. Red curtains, spotlights, blank verse, laughter, darkness, these are all confusedly superimposed in a messy image covered by one all-purpose word. We talk of the cinema killing the theatre, and in that phrase we refer to the theatre as it was when the cinema was born, a theatre of box office, foyer, tip-up seats, footlights, scene changes, intervals, music, as though the theatre was by very definition these and little more.

I will try to split the word four ways and distinguish four different meanings – and so will talk about a Deadly Theatre, a Holy Theatre, a Rough Theatre and an Immediate Theatre. Sometimes these four theatres really exist, standing side by side, in the West End of London, or in New York off Times Square. Sometimes they are hundreds of miles apart, the Holy in Warsaw and the Rough in Prague, and sometimes they are metaphoric: two of them mixing together within one evening, within one act. Sometimes within on single moment, the four of them, Holy, Rough, Immediate and Deadly intertwine.

The Deadly Theatre can at first sight be taken for granted, because it means bad theatre. As this is the form of theatre we see most often, and as it is most closely linked to the despised, much-attacked commercial theatre it might seem a waste of time to criticize it further. But it is only if we see that deadliness is deceptive and can appear anywhere, that we will become aware of the size of the problem.

The condition of the Deadly Theatre at least is fairly obvious. All through the world theatre audiences are dwindling. There are occasional new movements, good new writers and so on, but as a whole, the theatre not only fails to elevate or instruct, it hardly even entertains. The theatre has often been called a whore, meaning its art is impure, but today this is true in another sense – whores take the money and then go short on the pleasure. The Broadway crisis, the Paris crisis, the West End crisis are the same: we do not need the ticket agents to tell us that the theatre has become a deadly business and the public is smelling it out. In fact, were the public ever really to demand the true entertainment it talks about so often, we would almost all be hard put to know where to begin. A true theatre of joy is non-existent and it is not just the trivial comedy and the bad musical that fail to give us our money's worth – the Deadly Theatre finds its deadly way into grand opera and tragedy, into the plays of Molière and the plays of Brecht. Of course nowhere does the Deadly Theatre install itself so securely, so comfortably and so slyly as in the works of William Shakespeare. The Deadly Theatre takes easily to Shakespeare. We see his plays done by good actors in what seems like the proper way – they look lively and colourful, there is music and everyone is all dressed up, just as they are supposed to be in the best of classical theatres. Yet secretly we find it excruciatingly boring – and in our hearts we either blame Shakespeare, or theatre as such, or even ourselves. To make matters worse there is always a deadly spectator, who for special reasons enjoys a lack of intensity and even a lack of entertainment, such as the scholar who emerges from routine performances of the classics smiling because nothing has distracted him from trying over and confirming his pet theories to himself, whilst reciting his favourite lines under his breath. In his heart he sincerely wants a theatre that is nobler-than-life and he confuses a sort of intellectual satisfaction with the true experience for which he craves. Unfortunately, he lends the weight of his authority to dullness and so the Deadly Theatre goes on its way.

Anyone who watches the real successes as they appear each year, will see a very curious phenomenon. We expect the so-called hit to be livelier, faster, brighter than the flop – but this is not always the case. Almost every season in most theatre-loving towns, there is one great success that defies these rules; one play that succeeds not despite but because of dullness. After all, one associates culture with a certain sense of duty, historical costumes and long speeches with the sensation of being bored: so, conversely, just the right degree of boringness is a reassuring guarantee of a worthwhile event. Of course, the dosage is so subtle that it is impossible to establish the exact formula – too much and the audience is driven out of their seats, too little and it may find the theme too disagreeably intense. However, mediocre authors seem to feel their way unerringly to the perfect mixture – and they perpetuate the Deadly Theatre with dull successes, universally praised. Audiences crave for something in the theatre that they can term 'better' than life and for this reason are open to confuse culture, or the trappings of culture, with something they do not know, but sense obscurely could exist – so, tragically, in elevating something bad into a success they are only cheating themselves.

If we talk of deadly, let us note that the difference between life and death, so crystal clear in man, is somewhat veiled in other fields. A doctor can tell at once between the trace of life and the useless bag of bones that life has left; but we are less practised in observing how an idea, an attitude or a form can pass from the lively to the moribund. It is difficult to define but a child can smell it out. Let me give an example. In France there are two deadly ways of playing classical tragedy. One is traditional, and this involves using a special voice, a special manner, a noble look and an elevated musical delivery. The other way is no more than a half-hearted version of the same thing. Imperial gestures and royal values are fast disappearing from everyday life, so each new generation finds the grand manner more and more hollow, more and more meaningless. This leads the young actor to an angry and impatient search for what he calls truth. He wants to play his verse more realistically, to get it to sound like honest-to-God real speech, but he finds that the formality of the writing is so rigid that it resists this treatment. He is forced to an uneasy compromise that is neither refreshing, like ordinary talk, nor defiantly histrionic, like what we call ham. So his acting is weak and because ham is strong, it is remembered with a certain nostalgia. Inevitably, someone calls for tragedy to be played once again 'the way it is written'. This is fair enough, but unfortunately all the printed word can tell us is what was written on paper, not how it was once brought to life. There are no records, no tapes – only experts, but not one of them, of course, has firsthand knowledge. The real antiques have all gone – only some imitations have survived, in the shape of traditional actors, who continue to play in a traditional way, drawing their inspiration not from real sources, but from imaginary ones, such as the memory of the sound an older actor once made – a sound that in turn was a memory of a predecessor's way.

I once saw a rehearsal at the Comedie Française – a very young actor stood in front of a very old one and spoke and mimed the role with him like a reflection in a glass. This must not be confused with the great tradition, say, of the Noh actors passing knowledge orally from father to son. There it is meaning that is communicated – and meaning never belongs to the past. It can be checked in each man's own present experience. But to imitate the externals of acting only perpetuates manner – a manner hard to relate to anything at all.

Again with Shakespeare we hear or read the same advice – 'Play what is written'. But what is written? Certain ciphers on paper. Shakespeare's words are records of the words that he wanted to be spoken, words issuing as sounds from people's mouths, with pitch, pause, rhythm and gesture as part of their meaning. A word does not start as a word – it is an end product which begins as an impulse, stimulated by attitude and behaviour which dictate the need for expression. This process occurs inside the dramatist; it is repeated inside the actor. Both may only be conscious of the words, but both for the author and then for the actor the word is a small visible portion of a gigantic unseen formation. Some writers attempt to nail down their meaning and intentions in stage directions and explanations, yet we cannot help being struck by the fact that the best dramatists explain themselves the least. They recognize that further indications will most probably be useless. They recognize that the only way to find the true path to the speaking of a word is through a process that parallels the original creative one. This can neither be by-passed nor simplified. Unfortunately, the moment a lover speaks, or a king utters, we rush to give them a label: the lover is 'romantic', the king is 'noble' – and before we know it we are speaking of romantic love and kingly nobility or princeliness as though they are things we can hold in our hand and expect the actors to observe. But these are not substances and they do not exist. If we search for them, the best we can do is to make guesswork reconstructions from books and paintings. If you ask an actor to play in a 'romantic style' he will valiantly have a go, thinking he knows what you mean. What actually can he draw on? Hunch, imagination and a scrapbook of theatrical memories, all of which will give him a vague 'romanticness' that he will mix up with a disguised imitation of whatever older actor he happens to admire. If he digs into his own experiences the result may not marry with the text; if he just plays what he thinks is the text, it will be imitative and conventional. Either way the result is a compromise: at most times unconvincing.

It is vain to pretend that the words we apply to classical plays like 'musical', 'poetic', 'larger than life', 'noble', 'heroic', 'romantic', have any absolute meaning. They are the reflections of a critical attitude of a particular period, and to attempt to build a performance today to conform to these canons is the most certain road to deadly theatre – deadly theatre of a respectability that makes it pass as living truth.

Once, when giving a lecture on this theme, I was able to put it to a practical test. By luck, there was a woman in the audience who had neither read nor seen *King Lear*. I gave her Goneril's first speech and asked her to recite it as best she could for whatever values she found in it. She read it very simply – and the speech itself emerged full of eloquence and charm. I then explained that it was supposed to be the speech of a wicked woman and suggested her reading every word for hypocrisy. She tried to do so, and the audience saw what a hard unnatural wrestling with the simple music of the words was involved when she sought to act to a definition:

> Sir, I love you more than words can wield the matter;
> Dearer than eyesight, space, and liberty;
> Beyond that can be valued, rich or rare;
> No less than life, with grace, health, beauty, honour;
> As much as child e'er loved, or father found;
> A love that makes breath poor, and speech unable;
> Beyond all manner of so much I love you.

Anyone can try this for himself. Taste it on the tongue. The words are those of a lady of style and breeding accustomed to expressing herself in public, someone with ease and social aplomb. As for clues to her character, only the façade is presented and this, we see, is elegant and attractive. Yet if one thinks of the performances where Goneril speaks these first lines as a macabre villainess, and looks at the speech again, one is at a loss to know what suggests this – other than preconceptions of Shakespeare's moral attitudes. In fact, if Goneril in her first appearance does not play a 'monster', but merely what her given words suggest, then all the balance of the play changes – and in the subsequent scenes her villainy and Lear's martyrdom are neither as crude nor as simplified as they might appear. Of course, by the end of the play we learn that Goneril's actions make her what we call a monster – but a real monster, both complex and compelling.

In a living theatre, we would each day approach the rehearsal putting yesterday's discoveries to the test, ready to believe that the true play has once again escaped us. But the Deadly Theatre approaches the classics from the viewpoint that somewhere, someone has found out and defined how the play should be done.

This is the running problem of what we loosely call style.

Every work has its own style: it could not be otherwise: every period has its style. The moment we try to pinpoint this style we are lost. I remember vividly when shortly after the Pekin Opera had come to London a rival Chinese Opera Company followed, from Formosa. The Pekin Company was still in touch with its sources and creating its ancient patterns afresh each night: the Formosan company, doing the same items, was imitating its memories of them, skimping some details, exaggerating the showy passages, forgetting the meaning – nothing was reborn. Even in a strange exotic style the difference between life and death was unmistakable.

The real Pekin Opera was an example of a theatrical art where the outer forms do not change from generation to generation and only a few years ago it seemed as though it were so perfectly frozen that it could carry on for ever. To-day, even this superb relic has gone. Its force and its quality enabled it to survive way beyond its time, like a monument – but the day came when the gap between it and the life of the society around it became too great. The Red Guards reflect a different China. Few of the attitudes and meanings of the traditional Pekin Opera relate to the new structure of thought in which this people now lives. Today in Pekin the emperors and princesses have been replaced by landlords and soldiers, and the same incredible acrobatic skills are used to speak of very different themes. To the Westerner this seems a wicked shame and it is easy for us to shed cultivated tears. Of course, it is tragic that this miraculous heritage has been destroyed – and yet I feel that the ruthless Chinese attitude to one of their proudest possessions goes to the heart of the meaning of living theatre – theatre is always a self-destructive art, and it is always written on the wind. A professional theatre assembles different people every night and speaks to them through the language of behaviour. A performance gets set and usually has to be repeated – and repeated as well and accurately as possible – but from the day it is set something invisible is beginning to die.

In the Moscow Art Theatre, in Tel Aviv in the Habimah, productions have been kept going for forty years or more:

I have seen a faithful revival of Vakhtangov's twenties' staging of *Princess Turandot*; I have seen Stanislavsky's own work, perfectly preserved: but none of these had more than antiquarian interest, none had the vitality of new invention. At Stratford where we worry that we don't play our repertoire long enough to milk its full box office value, we now discuss this quite empirically: about five years, we agree, is the most a particular staging can live. It is not only the hairstyles, costumes and make-ups that look dated. All the different elements of staging – the shorthands of behaviour that stand for certain emotions; gestures, gesticulations and tones of voice – are all fluctuating on an invisible stock exchange all the time. Life is moving, influences are playing on actor and audience and other plays, other arts, the cinema, television, current events, join in the constant rewriting of history and the amending of the daily truth. In fashion houses someone will thump a table and say 'boots are definitely in': this is an existential fact. A living theatre that thinks it can stand aloof from anything so trivial as fashion will wilt. In the theatre, every form once born is mortal; every form must be reconceived, and its new conception will bear the marks of all the influences that surround it. In this sense, the theatre is relativity. Yet a great theatre is not a fashion house; perpetual elements do recur and certain fundamental issues underlie all dramatic activity. The deadly trap is to divide the eternal truths from the superficial variations; this is a subtle form of snobbery and it is fatal. For instance, it is accepted that scenery, costumes, music are fair game for directors and designers, and must in fact be renewed. When it comes to attitudes and behaviour we are much more confused, and tend to believe that these elements if true in the writing can continue to express themselves in similar ways.

Closely related to this is the conflict between theatre directors and musicians in opera productions where two totally different forms, drama and music, are treated as though they were one. A musician is dealing with a fabric that is as near as man can get to an expression of the invisible. His score notes this invisibility and his sound is made by instruments which hardly ever change. The player's personality is unimportant; a thin clarinettist can easily make a fatter sound than a fat one. The vehicle of music is separate from music itself. So the stuff of music comes and goes, always in the same way, free of the need to be revised and reassessed. But the vehicle of drama is flesh and blood and here completely different laws are at work. The vehicle and the message cannot be separated. Only a naked actor can begin to resemble a pure instrument like a violin and only if he has a completely classical physique, with neither paunch nor bandy legs. A ballet dancer is sometimes close to this condition and he can reproduce formal gestures unmodified by his own personality or by the outer movement of life. But the moment the actor dresses up and speaks with his own tongue he is entering the fluctuating territory of manifestation and existence that he shares with the spectator. Because the musician's experience is so different, he finds it hard to follow why the traditional bits of business that made Verdi laugh and Puccini slap his thighs seem neither funny nor illuminating today. Grand opera, of course, is the Deadly Theatre carried to absurdity. Opera is a nightmare of vast feuds over tiny details; of surrealist anecdotes that all turn round the same assertion: nothing needs to change. Everything in opera must change, but in opera change is blocked.

Again we must beware of indignation, for if we try to simplify the problem by making tradition the main barrier between ourselves and a living theatre we will again miss the real issue. There is a deadly element everywhere; in the cultural set-up, in our inherited artistic values, in the economic framework, in the actor's life, in the critic's function. As we examine these we will see that deceptively the opposite seems also true, for within the Deadly Theatre there are often tantalizing, abortive or even momentarily satisfying flickers of a real life.

In New York for instance, the most deadly element is certainly economic. This does not mean that all work done there is bad, but a theatre where a play for economic reasons rehearses for no more than three weeks is crippled at the outset.

Time is not the be-all and end-all: it is not impossible to get
an astonishing result in three weeks. Occasionally in the
theatre what one loosely calls chemistry, or luck, brings
about an astonishing rush of energy, and then invention follows invention in lightning chain reaction. But this is rare:
common sense shows that if the system rigidly excludes more
than three weeks' rehearsal most of the time, most things
suffer. No experimenting can take place, and no real artistic
risks are possible. The director must deliver the goods or be
fired and so must the actor. Of course time can also be used
very badly; it is possible to sit around for months discussing
and worrying and improvising without this showing in any
way whatsoever. I have seen Shakespearian productions in
Russia so conventional in approach that two full years of discussion and study of archives give no better a result than
scratch companies get in three weeks. I met an actor who rehearsed Hamlet for seven years and never played it because
the director died before it was finished. On the other hand,
productions of Russian plays rehearsed in the Stanislavsky
manner over years still reach a level of performance of which
we can only dream. The Berliner Ensemble uses time well,
they use it freely, spending about twelve months on a new
production, and over a number of years they have built up a
repertoire of shows, every one of which is remarkable – and
every one of which fills the theatre to capacity. In simple
capitalist terms, this is better business than the commercial
theatre where the scrambled and patched shows so seldom
succeed. Each season on Broadway or in London a large
number of expensive shows fold within a week or two against
the rare freak that scrapes through. None the less, the per-
centage of disasters hasn't jolted the system or the belief
that somehow it will all work out in the end. On Broadway
ticket prices are continually rising and, ironically, as each
season grows more disastrous, each season's hit makes more
money. As fewer and fewer people go through the doors,
larger and larger sums cross the ticket office counter, until
eventually one last millionaire will be paying a fortune for
one private performance for himself alone. So it comes about

that what is bad business for some is good business for others. Everyone moans and yet many want the system to go on.

The artistic consequences are severe. Broadway is not a jungle, it is a machine into which a great many parts snugly interlock. Yet each of these parts is brutalized; it has been deformed to fit and function smoothly. This is the only theatre in the world where every artist – by this, I mean designers, composers, lighting electricians, as well as actors – needs an agent for his personal protection. This sounds melodramatic, but in a sense everyone is continually in danger; his job, his reputation, his way of life is in daily balance. In theory, this tension should lead to an atmosphere of fear, and, were this the case, its destructiveness would be clearly seen. In practice, however, the underlying tension leads just as directly to the famous Broadway atmosphere, which is very emotional, throbbing with apparent warmth and good cheer. On the first day of rehearsal of *House of Flowers*, its composer Harold Arlen arrived wearing a blue cornflower, with champagne and presents for us all. As he hugged and kissed his way round the cast, Truman Capote who had written the libretto whispered darkly to me, 'It's love today. The lawyers'll be in tomorrow'. It was true. Pearl Bailey had served me with a 50,000-dollar writ before the show reached town. For a foreigner it was (in retrospect) all fun and exciting – everything is covered and excused by the term 'show business' – but in precise terms the brutal warmth directly relates to the lack of emotional finesse. In such conditions there is rarely the quiet and security in which anyone may dare expose himself. I mean the true unspectacular intimacy that long work and true confidence in other people brings about – on Broadway, a crude gesture of self-exposure is easy to come by, but this has nothing to do with the subtle, sensitive interrelation between people confidently working together. When the Americans envy the British, it is this odd sensibility, this uneven give and take that they mean. They call it style, and regard it as a mystery. When you cast a play in New York and you are told that a certain actor 'has style', this usually means an imitation of an imitation of a European. In the

American theatre, people talk seriously of style, as though this was a manner that could be acquired – and the actors who have played the classics and have been flattered by critics into believing that they have 'it', do everything to perpetuate the notion that style is a rare something that a few gentleman actors possess. Yet America could easily have a great theatre of its own. It possesses every one of the elements; there is a strength, courage, humour, cash and a capacity for facing hard facts.

One morning I stood in the Museum of Modern Art looking at the people swarming in for one dollar admission. Almost every one of them had the lively head and the individual look of a good audience – using the simple personal standard of an audience for whom one would like to do plays. In New York, potentially, there is one of the best audiences in the world. Unfortunately, it seldom goes to the theatre.

It seldom goes to the theatre because the prices are too high. Certainly it can afford these prices, but it has been let down too often. It is not for nothing that New York is the place where the critics are the most powerful and the toughest in the world. It is the audience, year after year, that has been forced to elevate simple fallible men into highly priced experts because, as when a collector buys an expensive work, he cannot afford to take the risk alone: the tradition of the expert valuers of works of art, like Duveen, has reached the box office line. So the circle is closed; not only the artists, but also the audience, have to have their protection men – and most of the curious, intelligent, nonconforming individuals stay away. This situation is not unique to New York. I had a closely related experience when we put on John Arden's *Sergeant Musgrave's Dance* in Paris at the Athenée. It was a true flop – almost all the Press was bad – and we were playing to virtually empty houses. Convinced that the play had an audience somewhere in the town, we announced that we would give three free performances. Such was the lure of complimentary tickets that they became like wild premières. Crowds fought to get in, the police had to draw iron grilles across the foyer, and the play itself went magnificently, as the actors, cheered by the warmth of the house, gave their best performance, which in turn earned them an ovation. The theatre which the night before had been a draughty morgue now hummed with the chatter and buzz of success. At the end, we put up the house lights and looked at the audience. Mostly young, they were all well dressed, rather formal, in suits and ties. Françoise Spira, directress of the theatre, came on the stage.

'Is there anyone here who could not afford the price of a ticket?'

One man put up his hand.

'And the rest of you, why did you have to wait to be let in for free?'

'It had a bad Press.'

'Do you believe the Press?'

Loud chorus of 'No!'

'Then, why. . . ?'

And from all sides the same answer – the risk is too great, too many disappointments. Here we see how the vicious circle is drawn. Steadily the Deadly Theatre digs its own grave.

Or else we can attack the problem the other way round. If good theatre depends on a good audience, then every audience has the theatre it deserves. Yet it must be very hard for spectators to be told of an audience's responsibility. How can this be faced in practice? It would be a sad day if people went to the theatre out of duty. Once within a theatre an audience cannot whip itself into being 'better' than it is. In a sense there is nothing a spectator can actually do. And yet there is a contradiction here that cannot be ignored, for everything depends on him.

When the Royal Shakespeare Company's production of *King Lear* toured through Europe the production was steadily improving and the best performances lay between Budapest and Moscow. It was fascinating to see how an audience composed largely of people with little knowledge of English could so influence a cast. These audiences brought

with them three things; a love for the play itself, real hunger
for a contact with foreigners and, above all, an experience
of life in Europe in the last years that enabled them to come
directly to the play's painful themes. The quality of the
attention that this audience brought expressed itself in silence
and concentration; a feeling in the house that affected the
actors as though a brilliant light were turned on their work.
As a result, the most obscure passages were illuminated;
they were played with a complexity of meaning and a fine
use of the English language that few of the audience could
literally follow, but which all could sense. The actors were
moved and excited and they proceeded to the United States,
prepared to give to an English-speaking audience all that this
focus had taught them. I was forced to go back to England
and only caught up with the company a few weeks later in
Philadelphia. To my surprise and dismay, much of the
quality had gone from their acting. I wanted to blame the
actors, but it was clear that they were trying as hard as they
could. It was the relation with the audience that had changed.
In Philadelphia, the audience understood English all right,
but this audience was composed largely of people who were
not interested in the play; people who came for all the conventional reasons – because it was a social event, because
their wives insisted, and so on. Undoubtedly, a way existed
to involve this particular audience in *King Lear*, but it was not
our way. The austerity of this production which had seemed
so right in Europe no longer made sense. Seeing people
yawn, I felt guilty, realizing that something else was demanded from us all. I knew that were I doing a production of
King Lear for the people of Philadelphia I would without
condescension stress everything differently – and, in immediate terms, I would get it to work better. But with an established production on tour I could do nothing. The actors,
however, were instinctively responding to the new situation.
They were underlining everything in the play that could
arrest the spectator – that is to say, when there was a bit of
exciting action or a burst of melodrama, they exploited it,
they played louder and cruder and of course whipped past

those intricate passages that the non-English audience had so enjoyed – which, ironically, only an English-speaking audience could have appreciated to the full. Eventually our impressario took the play to the Lincoln Centre in New York – a giant auditorium where the acoustics were bad and the audience resented its poor contact with the stage. We were put in this vast theatre for economic reasons: a simple illustration of how a closed circle of cause and effect is produced, so that the wrong audience or the wrong place or both conjures from the actors their coarsest work. Again, the actors, responding to the given conditions, had no choice, they faced the front, spoke loudly and quite rightly threw away all that had become precious in their work. This danger is built into every tour, because in a sense few of the conditions of the original performance apply – and contact with each new audience is often a matter of luck. In the old days, the strolling players naturally adapted their work to each new place: elaborate modern productions have no such flexibility. In fact, when we played 'US', the Royal Shakespeare Theatre's group-happening-collaborative spectacle on the Vietnam war, we decided to refuse all invitations to tour. Every element in it had come into being just for the particular cross-section of London that sat in the Aldwych Theatre in 1966. The fact that we had no text wrought and set by a dramatist was the condition of this particular experiment. Contact with the audience, through shared references, became the substance of the evening. Had we a shaped text, we could have played in other places, without one we were like a happening – and in the event, we all felt that something was lost in playing it even through a London season of five months. One performance would have been the true culmination. We made the mistake of feeling obligated to enter our own repertoire. A repertoire repeats, and to repeat something must be fixed. The rules of British censorship prevent actors adapting and improvising in performance. So in this case, the fixing was the beginning of a slide towards the deadly – the liveliness of the actors waned as the immediacy of the relation with their public and their theme lessened.

During a talk to a group at a university I once tried to illustrate how an audience affects actors by the quality of its attention. I asked for a volunteer. A man came forward, and I gave him a sheet of paper on which was typed a speech from Peter Weiss's play about Auschwitz, *The Investigation*. The section was a description of bodies inside a gas chamber. As the volunteer took the paper and read it over to himself the audience tittered in the way an audience always does when it sees one of its kind on the way to making a fool of himself. But the volunteer was too struck and too appalled by what he was reading to react with the sheepish grins that are also customary. Something of his seriousness and concentration reached the audience and it fell silent. Then at my request he began to read out loud. The very first words were loaded with their own ghastly sense and the reader's response to them. Immediately the audience understood. It became one with him, with the speech – the lecture room and the volunteer who had come on to the platform vanished from sight – the naked evidence from Auschwitz was so powerful that it took over completely. Not only did the reader continue to speak in a shocked attentive silence, but his reading, technically speaking, was perfect – it had neither grace nor lack of grace, skill nor lack of skill – it was perfect because he had no attention to spare for self-consciousness, for wondering whether he was using the right intonation. He knew the audience wanted to hear, and he wanted to let them hear: the images found their own level and guided his voice unconsciously to the appropriate volume and pitch.

After this, I asked for another volunteer, and gave him the speech from *Henry V* which lists the names and numbers of the French and English dead. When he read this aloud, all the faults of the amateur actor appeared. One look at the volume of Shakespeare had already set off a series of conditioned reflexes to do with speaking verse. He put on a false voice that strived to be noble and historical, mouthed his words roundly, made awkward stresses, got tongue-tied, stiff, and confused, and the audience listened inattentive and restless. When he had done, I asked the audience why they could not take the list of dead at Agincourt as seriously as the description of death at Auschwitz. This provoked a lively exchange.

'Agincourt's in the past.'

'But Auschwitz is in the past.'

'Only fifteen years.'

'So how long's it got to take?'

'When's a corpse a historical corpse?'

'How many years make killing romantic?'

After this had gone on for some time, I proposed an experiment. The amateur actor was to read the speech again, stopping for a moment after each name: the audience was to endeavour silently in the pause to recall and put together its impressions of Auschwitz and Agincourt, to try to find a way of believing that these names were once individuals, as vividly as if the butchery had occurred in living memory. The amateur began to read again and the audience worked hard, playing its part. As he spoke the first name, the half silence became a dense one. Its tension caught the reader, there was an emotion in it, shared between him and them and it turned all his attention away from himself on to the subject matter he was speaking. Now the audience's concentration began to guide him: his inflexions were simple, his rhythms true: this in turn increased the audience's interest and so the two-way current began to flow. When this was ended, no explanations were needed, the audience had seen itself in action, it had seen how many layers silence can contain.

Of course, like all experiments, this was an artificial one: here, the audience was given an unusually active role and as a result it directed an inexperienced actor. Usually, an experienced actor reading a passage like this will impose a silence on an audience that is in proportion to the degree of truth he brings to it. Occasionally, an actor can completely dominate any house, and so, like a master matador, he can work the audience the way he pleases. Usually, however, this cannot come from the stage alone. For instance, both the actors and myself found *The Visit* and *Marat/Sade* more rewarding to play in America than in England. The English

refused to take *The Visit* on its own terms; the story told of
the ruthlessness latent in any small community, and when
we played in the English provinces, to virtually empty
houses, the reaction of those who came was 'it's not real', 'it
couldn't happen', and they enjoyed it or disliked it on the
level of fantasy. The *Marat/Sade* was liked in London not so
much as a play about revolution, war and madness as a display of theatricality. The opposing words 'literary' and
'theatrical' have many meanings, but in the English theatre,
when used as praise, they all too often describe ways of
warding off contact with disturbing themes. The American
audience reacted to both plays much more directly, they
accepted and believed the propositions that man is greedy
and murderous, a potential lunatic. They were caught and
held by the material of the drama, and in the case of *The
Visit* they often did not even comment on the fact that the
story was being told to them in a somewhat unfamiliar,
expressionistic way. They simply discussed what the play
had said. The great Kazan–Williams–Miller hits, Albee's
Virginia Woolf, summoned audiences that met the cast in the
true shared territory of theme and concern – and they were
powerful events, the circle of performance was riveting and
complete.

   In America, in powerful waves, comes a recognition of the
deadly, and a strong reaction against it. Years ago, the Actors'
Studio came into being to give a faith and continuity to those
unhappy artists who were being so rapidly thrown in and out
of work. Basing a very serious and systematic study on a
portion of Stanislavsky's teaching, the Actors' Studio developed a very remarkable school of acting that corresponded
perfectly to the needs of the playwrights and public of the
time. Actors still had to give results in three weeks, but they
were sustained by the school's tradition and they did not
come empty-handed to the first rehearsal. This background
of teaching gave a strength and integrity to their work. The
Method Actor was trained to reject cliché imitations of
reality and to search for something more real in himself. He
then had to present this through the living of it, and so acting

became a deeply naturalistic study. 'Reality' is a word with many meanings, but here it was understood to be that slice of the real that reflected the people and the problems around the actor, and it coincided with the slices of existence that the writers of the day, Miller, Tennessee Williams, Inge, were trying to define. In much the same way Stanislavsky's theatre drew its strength from the fact that it corresponded to the needs of the best Russian classics, all of which were cast in a naturalistic form. For a number of years in Russia, the school, the public and the play had made a coherent whole. Then Meyerhold challenged Stanislavsky, proposing a different style of playing, in order to capture other elements of 'reality'. But Meyerhold disappeared. In America today, the time is ripe for a Meyerhold to appear, since naturalistic representations of life no longer seems to Americans adequate to express the forces that drive them. Now Genet is discussed, Shakespeare re-evaluated, Artaud quoted: there is a lot of talk about ritual: and all this for very realistic reasons, as many concrete aspects of American living can only be captured along these lines. Just a short time ago, the English were full of envy for the vitality of the American theatre. Now the pendulum swings towards London, as though the English hold all the keys. Years ago I saw a girl at the Actors' Studio approaching a speech of Lady Macbeth's by pretending to be a tree: when I described this in England it sounded comic, and even today many English actors have yet to discover why odd-sounding exercises are so necessary. In New York, however, the girl did not need to learn about group work and improvisations, she had accepted these, and she needed to understand about the meaning and demands of form; standing with her arms in the air trying to 'feel', she was pouring her ardour and energy uselessly in the wrong direction.

All this brings us back to the same problem. The word theatre has many sloppy meanings. In most of the world, the theatre has no exact place in society, no clear purpose, it only exists in fragments: one theatre chases money, another chases glory, another chases emotion, another chases politics, another chases fun. The actor is bundled from pillar to post – confused and consumed by conditions outside his control. Actors may sometimes seem jealous or trivial, yet I have never known an actor who did not want to work. This wish to work is his strength. It is what enables professionals everywhere to understand each other. But he cannot reform his profession alone. In a theatre with few schools and no aims, he is usually the tool, not the instrument. Yet when the theatre does come back to the actor, the problem is still not solved. On the contrary, deadly acting becomes the heart of the crisis.

The dilemma of the actor is not unique to commercial theatres with inadequate rehearsal time. Singers and often dancers keep their teachers by them to the end of their days: actors once launched have nothing whatsoever to help them to develop their talents. If this is seen most alarmingly in the commercial theatre, the same applies to permanent companies. After he reaches a certain position the actor does no more homework. Take a young actor, unformed, undeveloped, but bursting with talent, full of latent possibilities. Quite rapidly he discovers what he can do, and, after mastering his initial difficulties, with a bit of luck he may find himself in the enviable position of having a job which he loves, doing it well while getting paid and admired at the same time. If he is to develop, the next stage must be to go beyond his apparent range, and to begin to explore what really comes hard. But no one has time for this sort of problem. His friends are little use, his parents are unlikely to know much about his art, and his agent, who may be well-meaning and intelligent, is not there to guide him past good offers of good parts towards a vague something else that would be even better. Building a career and artistic development do not necessarily go hand in hand; often the actor, as his career grows, begins to turn in work that gets more and more similar. It is a wretched story, and all the exceptions blur the truth.

How does the average actor spend his days? Of course, it's a wide range: from lying in bed, drinking, going to the hairdresser, to the agent, filming, recording, reading, sometimes studying; even, latterly, toying a bit with politics. But whether his use of time is frivolous or earnest is beside the point: little that he does relates to his main preoccupation – not to stand still as an actor – which means not to stand still as a human being, which means work aimed at his artistic growth – and where can such work take place? Time after time I have worked with actors who after the usual preamble that they 'put themselves in my hands' are tragically incapable however hard they try of laying down for one brief instant even in rehearsal the image of themselves that has hardened round an inner emptiness. On the occasions that it is possible to penetrate this shell, it is like smashing the picture on a television set.

In England, it seems suddenly that we have a marvellous new breed of young actors – we feel we are witnessing two lines of men in a factory facing opposite directions: one line shuffles out grey, tired, the other strides forward fresh and vital. We get the impression that one line is better than the other, that the lively line is made of better stock. This is partly true, but in the end the new shift will be as tired and grey as the old; it is an inevitable result of certain conditions that have not yet changed. The tragedy is that the professional status of actors over the age of 30 is seldom a true reflection of their talents. There are countless actors who never have the chance to develop their inborn potential to its proper fruition. Naturally, in an individualist profession, false and exaggerated importance is given to exceptional cases. Outstanding actors like all real artists have some mysterious psychic chemistry, half conscious and yet three-quarters hidden, that they themselves may only define as 'instinct', 'hunch', 'my voices', that enables them to develop their vision and their art. Special cases may follow special rules: one of the greatest actresses of our time who seems in rehearsal to be observing no method whatsoever actually has an extraordinary system of her own which she can only articulate in nursery language. 'Kneading the flour today, darling,' she has said to me. 'Putting it back to bake a bit longer', 'Need some yeast now', 'We're basting this morning'. No matter: this is precise science, just as much as if she gave it the terminology of the Actors' Studio. But her ability to get results stays with her alone: she cannot communicate it in any useful way to the people around her, so while she is 'cooking her pie' and the next actor is just 'doing it the way he feels it,' and the third in drama school language, is 'searching for the Stanislavskian super-objective', no real working-together between them all is possible. It has long been recognized that without a permanent company few actors can thrive indefinitely. However, it must also be faced that even a permanent company is doomed to deadliness in the long run if it is without an aim, and thus without a method, and thus without a school. And by a school, naturally I don't mean a gymnasium where the actor exercises his limbs in limbo. Flexing muscles alone cannot develop an art; scales don't make a pianist nor does fingerwork help a painter's brush: yet a great pianist practises finger exercises for many hours a day, and Japanese painters spend their lives practising to draw a perfect circle. The art of acting is in some ways the most exacting one of all, and without constant schooling, the actor will stop half-way.

So when we find deadliness, who is the culprit? Enough has been said publicly and privately to make the critics' ears burn, to make us believe that it is from them that the worst deadliness really stems. Over the years we moan and grumble about 'the Critics' as though it were always the same six men hurtling by jet, from Paris to New York, from art show to concert to the play, always committing the same monumental errors. Or as though they were all like Thomas à Becket – the jolly, whoring friend of the King who the day he became Cardinal turned as disapproving as all his predecessors: critics come and go, yet those who are criticized generally find 'them' the same. Our system, the newspapers, the reader's demands, the notice dictated by phone, the problems of space, the quantity of rubbish in our playhouses, the soul-destroying effect of doing the same job often and too long, all conspire to prevent a critic from exercising his vital function. When the man in the street goes to the theatre he can claim just to serve his own pleasure. When a critic goes to a play, he can say he is just serving the man in the street, but it is not accurate. He is not just a tipster. A critic has a far more important role, an essential one, in fact, for an art without critics would be constantly menaced by far greater dangers.

For instance, a critic is always serving the theatre when he is hounding out incompetence. If he spends most of his time grumbling, he is almost always right. The appalling difficulty of making theatre must be accepted: it is, or would be, if truly practised, perhaps the hardest medium of all: it is merciless, there is no room for error, or for waste. A novel can survive the reader who skips pages, or entire chapters; the audience, apt to change from pleasure to boredom in a wink can be lost, irrevocably. Two hours is a short time and an eternity: to use two hours of public time is a fine art. Yet this art with its frightening exigencies is served largely by casual labour. In a deadly vacuum there are few places where we can properly learn the arts of the theatre – so we tend to drop in on the theatre offering love instead of science. This is what the unfortunate critic is nightly called to judge.

Incompetence is the vice, the condition and the tragedy of the world's theatre on any level: for every good light comedy or musical or political revue or verse play or classic that we see there are scores of others that most of the time are betrayed by a lack of elementary skills. The techniques of staging, designing, speaking, walking across a stage, sitting – even listening – just aren't sufficiently known; compare the little it takes – except luck – to get work in many of the theatres of the world with the minimum level of skill demanded say in piano playing: think of how many thousands of music teachers in thousands of small cities can play all the notes of the most difficult passages of Liszt or sight-read Scriabin. Compared with the simple ability of musicians most of our work is at amateur level most of the time. A critic will see far more incompetence than competence in his theatregoing. I was once asked to direct an opera at a Middle Eastern opera house which wrote frankly in its letter of invitation 'our orchestra has not all the instruments and plays some wrong notes but our audiences so far have not noticed'. Fortunately, the critic does tend to notice and in this sense, his angriest reaction is valuable – it is a call for competence. This is a vital function, but he has still another one. He is a pathmaker.

The critic joins in the deadly game when he does not accept this responsibility, when he belittles his own importance. A critic is usually a sincere and decent man acutely aware of the human aspects of his job; one of the famous 'Butchers of Broadway' was said to have been tormented by the knowledge that on him alone depended people's happiness and future. Still, even if he is aware of his power of destruction, he underrates his power for good. When the *status quo* is rotten – and few critics anywhere would dispute this – the only possibility is to judge events in relation to a possible goal. This goal should be the same for artist and critic – the moving towards a less deadly, but, as yet, largely undefined theatre. This is our eventual purpose, our shared aim, and noting all the sign-posts and footprints on the way is our common task. Our relations with critics may be strained in a superficial sense: but in a deeper one the relationship is absolutely necessary: like the fish in the ocean, we need one another's devouring talents to perpetuate the sea bed's existence. However, this devouring is not nearly enough: we need to share the endeavour to rise to the surface. This is what is hard for all of us. The critic is part of the whole and whether he writes his notices fast or slow, short or long, is not really important. Has he an image of how a theatre could be in his community and is he revising this image around each experience he receives? How many critics see their job this way?

It is for this reason that the more the critic becomes an insider, the better. I see nothing but good in a critic plunging into our lives, meeting actors, talking, discussing, watching, intervening. I would welcome his putting his hands on the medium and attempting to work it himself. Certainly, there is a tiny social problem – how does a critic talk to someone whom he has just damned in print? Momentary awkwardnesses may arise – but it is ludicrous to think that it is largely this that deprives some critics of a vital contact with the work of which they are a part. The embarrassment on his side and ours can easily be lived down and certainly a closer relation with the work will in no way put the critic into the position of connivance with the people he has got to know. The criticism that theatre people make of one another is usually of devastating severity – but absolutely precise. The critic who no longer enjoys the theatre is obviously a deadly critic, the critic who loves the theatre but is not critically clear what this means, is also a deadly critic: the vital critic is the critic who has clearly formulated for himself what the theatre could be – and who is bold enough to throw this formula into jeopardy each time he participates in a theatrical event.

The worst problem for the professional critic is that he is seldom asked to expose himself to scorching events that change his thinking: it is hard for him to retain his enthusiasm, when there are few good plays anywhere in the world. Year after year, there is rich new material pouring into the cinema; yet all the theatres can do is make an unhappy choice between great traditional writing or far less good modern works. We are now in another area of the problem, also considered to be central: the dilemma of the deadly writer.

It is woefully difficult to write a play. A playwright is required by the very nature of drama to enter into the spirit of opposing characters. He is not a judge; he is a creator – and even if his first attempt at drama concerns only two people, whatever the style he is still required to live fully with them both. The job of shifting oneself totally from one character to another – a principle on which all of Shakespeare and all of Chekhov is built – is a super-human task at any time. It takes unique talents and perhaps ones that do not even correspond with our age. If the work of the beginner-playwright often seems thin, it may well be because his range of human sympathy is still unstretched – on the other hand, nothing seems more suspect than the mature middle-aged man of letters who sits down to invent characters and then tell us all their secrets. The French revulsion against the classic form of the novel was a reaction from the omniscience of the author: if you ask Marguerite Duras what her character is feeling she will often reply, 'How do I know?'; if you ask Robbe Grillet why a character has made a certain action he could answer, 'All I know for sure is that he opened the door with his right hand'. But this way of thinking hasn't reached the French theatre, where it is still the author who at the first rehearsal does a one-man show, reading out and performing all the parts. This is the most exaggerated form of a tradition that dies hard everywhere. The author has been forced to make a virtue of his specialness, and to turn his literariness into a crutch for a self-importance that in his heart he knows is not justified by his work. Maybe a need for privacy is a deep part of an author's make-up. It is possible that it is only with the door closed, communing with himself, that he can wrestle into form inner images and conflicts of which he would never speak in public. We do not know how Aeschylus or Shakespeare worked. All we know is that gradually the relationship between the man who sits at home working it all out on paper and the world of actors and stages is getting more and more tenuous, more and more unsatisfactory. The best English writing is coming out of the theatre itself: Wesker, Arden, Osborne, Pinter, to take obvious examples, are all directors and actors as well as authors – and at times they even have been involved as impresarios.

None the less, whether scholar or actor, too few authors are what we could truly call inspiring or inspired. If the author were a master and not a victim one could say that he had betrayed the theatre. As it is, one can say that he is betraying by omission – the authors are failing to rise to the challenge of their times. Of course, there are exceptions, brilliant, startling ones, here and there. But I am thinking again of the quantity of new creative work poured into films compared with the world's output of new dramatic texts. When new plays set out to imitate reality, we are more conscious of what is imitative

than what is real: if they explore character, it is seldom that
they go far beyond stereotypes; if it is argument they offer,
it is seldom that argument is taken to arresting extremes;
even if it is a quality of life that they wish to evoke, we are
usually offered no more than the literary quality of the well-
turned phrase; if it is social criticism they are after, it seldom
touches the heart of any social target; if they wish for laughter, it is usually by well-worn means.

As a result, we are often forced to choose between reviving
old plays or staging new plays which we find inadequate, just
as a gesture towards the present day. Or else to attempt to
initiate a play – as, for example, when a group of actors and
writers in the Royal Shakespeare Theatre, wanting a play on
Vietnam that did not exist, set out to make one, using techniques of improvisation and authorless invention to fill the
vacuum. Group creation can be infinitely richer, if the group
is rich, than the product of weak individualism – yet it proves
nothing. There is eventually a need for authorship to reach
the ultimate compactness and focus that collective work is
almost obliged to miss.

In theory few men are as free as a playwright. He can bring
the whole world on to his stage. But in fact he is strangely
timid. He looks at the whole of life, and like all of us he only
sees a tiny fragment; a fragment, one aspect of which catches
his fancy. Unfortunately he rarely searches to relate his detail
to any larger structure – it is as though he accepts without
question his intuition as complete, his reality as all of reality.
It is as though his belief in his subjectivity as his instrument
and his strength precludes him from any dialectic between
what he sees and what he apprehends. So there is either the
author who explores his inner experience in depth and darkness, or else the author who shuns these areas, exploring the
outside world – each one thinks his world is complete. If
Shakespeare had never existed we would quite understandably
theorize that the two can never combine. The Elizabethan
Theatre did exist, though – and awkwardly enough we
have this example constantly hanging over our heads. Four
hundred years ago it was possible for a dramatist to wish

to bring the pattern of events in the outside world, the inner events of complex men isolated as individuals, the vast tug of their fears and aspirations into open conflict. Drama was exposure, it was confrontation, it was contradiction and it led to analysis, involvement, recognition and, eventually, to an awakening of understanding. Shakespeare was not a peak without a base, floating magically on a cloud: he was supported by scores of lesser dramatists, naturally with lesser and lesser talents – but sharing the same ambition for wrestling with what Hamlet calls the forms and pressures of the age. Yet a neo–Elizabethan theatre based on verse and pageantry would be a monstrosity. This compels us to look at the problem more closely and try to find out what exactly the special Shakespeare qualities are. One simple fact emerges at once. Shakespeare used the same unit that is available today – a few hours of public time. He used this time span to cram together, second for second, a quantity of lively material of incredible richness. This material exists simultaneously on an infinite variety of levels, it plunges deep and reaches high: the technical devices, the use of verse and prose, the many changing scenes, exciting, funny, disturbing, were the ones the author was compelled to develop to satisfy his needs: and the author had a precise, human and social aim which gave him reason for searching for his themes, reason for searching for his means, reason for making theatre. We see the present-day author still locked in the prisons of anecdote, consistency and style, conditioned by the relics of Victorian values to think ambition and pretension dirty words. How desperately he needs both. If only he were ambitious, if only he were to comb the sky! For as long as he is an ostrich, an isolated ostrich, this can never happen. Before he can raise his head he too must face the same crisis. He too must discover what he believes a theatre to be.

Naturally, an author can only work with what he has got and cannot leap out of his sensibility. He cannot talk himself into being better or other than he is. He can only write about what he sees and thinks and feels. But one thing can amend the instrument at his disposal. The more clearly he recognizes the missing links in his relationships – the more accurately he experiences that he is never deep enough in enough aspects of life, nor deep enough in enough aspects of the theatre, that his necessary seclusion is also his prison – the more then can he begin to find ways of connecting strands of observation and experience which at present remain unlinked.

Let me try to define more precisely the issue that confronts the writer. The theatre's needs have changed, yet the difference is not simply one of fashion. It is not as though fifty years ago one type of theatre was in vogue while today the author who feels the 'pulse of the public' can find his way to the new idiom. The difference is that for a long time playwrights have very successfully traded on applying to the theatre values from other fields. If a man could 'write' – and writing meant the ability to put together words and phrases in a stylish and elegant manner – then this was accepted as a start towards good writing in the theatre. If a man could invent a good plot, good twists, or what's described as 'understanding human nature' these were all considered to be at least stepping-stones towards fine playwriting. Now the lukewarm virtues of good craftsmanship, sound construction, effective curtains, crisp dialogue have all been thoroughly debunked. Not least, the influences of television has been to accustom viewers of all classes all over the world to make instant judgment – at the moment they catch sight of a shot on the screen – so that the average adult continually situates scenes and characters unaided, without a 'good craftsman' helping with exposition and explanation. The steady discrediting of non-theatre virtues is now beginning to clear the way for other virtues. These are in fact more closely related to the theatre form and also they are more exacting ones. Because if one starts from the premise that a stage is a stage – not a convenient place for the unfolding of a staged novel or a staged poem or a staged lecture or a staged story – then the word that is spoken on this stage exists, or fails to exist, only in relation to the tensions it creates on that stage within the given stage circumstances. In other words, although the dramatist brings his own life nurtured by the life around him into his work – the empty stage is no ivory tower – the choices he makes and the values he observes are only powerful in proportion to what they create in the language of theatre. Many examples of this can be seen wherever an author for moral or political reasons attempts to use a play as the bearer of a message. Whatever the value of this message, in the end it only works according to values that belong to the stage itself. An author today can easily cheat himself if he thinks that he can 'use' a conventional form as a vehicle. This was true when conventional forms still had life for their audience. Today when no conventional forms stand up any more, even the author who doesn't care about theatre as such, but only about what he is trying to say, is compelled to begin at the root – by facing the problem of the very nature of dramatic utterance. There is no way out – unless he is prepared to settle for a second-hand vehicle that's no longer in working order and very unlikely to take him to where he wants to go. Here the author's real problem and the director's real problem go hand in glove.

When I hear a director speaking glibly of serving the author, of letting a play speak for itself, my suspicions are aroused, because this is the hardest job of all. If you just let a play speak, it may not make a sound. If what you want is for the play to be heard, then you must conjure its sound from it. This demands many deliberate actions and the result may have great simplicity. However, setting out to 'be simple' can be quite negative, an easy evasion of the exacting steps to the simple answer.

It is a strange role, that of the director: he does not ask to be God and yet his role implies it. He wants to be fallible, and yet an instinctive conspiracy of the actors is to make him the arbiter, because an arbiter is so desperately wanted all the time. In a sense the director is always an imposter, a guide at night who does not know the territory, and yet he has no choice – he must guide, learning the route as he goes. Deadliness often lies in wait when he does not recognize this situation, and hopes for the best, when it is the worst that he needs to face.

Deadliness always brings us back to repetition: the deadly director uses old formulae, old methods, old jokes, old effects; stock beginnings to scenes, stock ends; and this applies equally to his partners, the designers and composers, if they do not start each time afresh from the void, the desert and the true question – why clothes at all, why music, what for? A deadly director is a director who brings no challenge to the conditioned reflexes that every department must contain.

For half a century at least, it has been accepted that the theatre is a unity and that all elements should try to blend – this has led to the emergence of the director. But it has largely been a matter of external unity, a fairly external blending of styles so that contradictory styles do not jar. When we consider how the inner unity of a complex work can be expressed we may find quite the reverse – that a jarring of externals is quite essential. When we go further and consider the audience – and the society from which the audience comes – the true unity of all these elements may best be served by factors that by other standards seem ugly, discordant and destructive.

A stable and harmonious society might need only to look for ways of reflecting and reaffirming its harmony in its theatres. Such theatres could set out to unite cast and audience in a mutual 'yes'. But a shifting, chaotic world often must choose between a playhouse that offers a spurious 'yes' or a provocation so strong that it splinters its audience into fragments of vivid 'nos'.

*　*　*

Lecturing on these themes has taught me a great deal. I know that at this point someone always leaps up in the audience to ask whether (a) I think that all theatres that are not up to the loftiest standards should be closed or (b) whether I think it's a bad thing for people to enjoy themselves at a good entertainment or (c) what about the amateurs?

My reply usually is that I would never like to be a censor, ban anything or spoil anyone's fun. I have the greatest regard for the repertory theatres, and for groups all through the world struggling against great odds to sustain the level of their work. I have the greatest respect for other people's pleasure and particularly for anyone's frivolity. I came to the theatre myself for sensual and often irresponsible reasons. Entertainment is fine. But I still ask my questioners whether they really feel on the whole that theatres give them what they expect or want.

I don't particularly mind waste, but I think it's a pity not to know what one is wasting. Some old ladies use pound notes as bookmarks: this is only silly if it is absent-minded.

The problem of the Deadly Theatre is like the problem of the deadly bore. Every deadly bore has head, heart, arms, legs: usually, he has family and friends: he even has his admirers. Yet we sigh when we come across him – and in this sigh we are regretting that somehow he is at the bottom instead of the top of his possibilities. When we say deadly, we never mean dead: we mean something depressingly active, but for this very reason capable of change. The first step towards this change is facing the simple unattractive fact that most of what is called theatre anywhere in the world is a travesty of a word once full of sense. War or peace, the colossal bandwagon of culture trundles on, carrying each artist's traces to the evermounting garbage heap. Theatres, actors, critics and public are interlocked in a machine that creaks, but never stops. There is always a new season in hand and we are too busy to ask the only vital question which measures the whole structure. Why theatre at all? What for? Is it an anachronism, a superannuated oddity, surviving like an old monument or a quaint custom? Why do we applaud, and what? Has the stage a real place in our lives? What function can it have? What could it serve? What could it explore? What are its special properties?

In Mexico, before the wheel was invented, gangs of slaves had to carry giant stones through the jungle and up the mountains, while their children pulled their toys on tiny rollers. The slaves made the toys, but for centuries failed to make the connection. When good actors play in bad comedies or second-rate musicals, when audiences applaud indifferent classics because they enjoy just the costumes or just the way the sets change, or just the prettiness of the leading actress, there is nothing wrong. But none the less, have they noticed what is underneath the toy they are dragging on a string? It's a wheel.

2

The Holy Theatre

I AM calling it the Holy Theatre for short, but it could be called The Theatre of the Invisible – Made – Visible: the notion that the stage is a place where the invisible can appear has a deep hold on our thoughts. We are all aware that most of life escapes our senses: a most powerful explanation of the various arts is that they talk of patterns which we can only begin to recognize when they manifest themselves as rhythms or shapes. We observe that the behaviour of people, of crowds, of history, obeys such recurrent patterns. We hear that trumpets destroyed the walls of Jericho, we recognize that a magical thing called music can come from men in white ties and tails, blowing, waving, thumping and scraping away. Despite the absurd means that produce it, through the concrete in music we recognize the abstract, we understand that ordinary men and their clumsy instruments are transformed by an art of possession. We may make a personality cult of the conductor, but we are aware that he is not really making the music, it is making him – if he is relaxed, open and attuned, then the invisible will take possession of him; through him, it will reach us.

This is the notion, the true dream behind the debased ideals of the Deadly Theatre. This is what is meant and remembered by those who with feeling and seriousness use big hazy words like nobility, beauty, poetry, which I would like to re-examine for the particular quality they suggest. The theatre is the last forum where idealism is still an open question: many audiences all over the world will answer positively from their own experience that they have seen the face of the invisible through an experience on the stage that transcended their experience in life. They will maintain that

Oedipus or *Berenice* or *Hamlet* or *The Three Sisters* performed
with beauty and with love fires the spirit and gives them a
reminder that daily drabness is not necessarily all. When
they reproach the contemporary theatre for its kitchen sinks
and cruelties, this, honourably, is what they are trying to say.
They remember how during the war the romantic theatre,
the theatre of colours and sounds, of music and movement,
came like water to the thirst of dry lives. At that time, it was
called escape and yet the word was only partially accurate. It
was an escape, but also a reminder: a sparrow in a prison cell.
When the war was over, the theatre again strove even more
vigorously to find the same values.

The theatre of the late '40s had many glories: it was the
theatre of Jouvet and Bérard, and of Jean-Louis Barrault, of
Clavé at the ballet, *Don Juan*, *Amphitryon*, *La Folle de
Chaillot*, *Carmen*, John Gielgud's revival of '*The Importance of
Being Ernest*, *Peer Gynt* at the Old Vic, Olivier's *Oedipus*,
Olivier's *Richard III*, *The Lady's not for Burning*, *Venus
Observed*; of Massine at Covent Garden under the birdcage
in the *The Three-Cornered Hat* just as he had been fifteen years
before – this was a theatre of colour and movement, of fine
fabrics, of shadows, of eccentric, cascading words, of leaps of
thought and of cunning machines, of lightness and of all
forms of mystery and surprise – it was the theatre of a battered Europe that seemed to share one aim – a reaching back
towards a memory of lost grace.

Walking along the Reeperbahn in Hamburg on an afternoon in 1946, whilst a damp dispiriting grey mist whirled
round the desperate mutilated tarts, some on crutches, noses
mauve, cheeks hollow, I saw a crowd of children pushing excitedly into a night club door. I followed them. On the stage
was a bright blue sky. Two seedy, spangled clowns sat on a
painted cloud on their way to visit the Queen of Heaven.
'What shall we ask her for?' said one. 'Dinner,' said the other
and the children screamed approval. 'What shall we have for
dinner?' 'Schinken, leberwurst . . .' the clown began to list
all the unobtainable foods and the squeals of excitement were
gradually replaced by a hush – a hush that settled into a deep

and true theatrical silence. An image was being made real, in answer to the need for something that was not there.

In the burnt-out shell of the Hamburg Opera only the stage itself remained – but an audience assembled on it whilst against the back wall on a wafer-thin set singers clambered up and down to perform *The Barber of Seville*, because nothing would stop them doing so. In a tiny attic fifty people crammed together while in the inches of remaining space a handful of the best actors resolutely continued to practise their art. In a ruined Düsseldorf, a minor Offenbach about smugglers and bandits filled the theatre with delight. There was nothing to discuss, nothing to analyse – in Germany that winter, as in London a few years before, the theatre was responding to a hunger. What, however, was this hunger? Was it a hunger for the invisible, a hunger for a reality deeper than the fullest form of everyday life – or was it a hunger for the missing things of life, a hunger, in fact, for buffers against reality? The question is an important one, because many people believe that in the very recent past there still was a theatre with certain values, certain skills, certain arts that we perhaps wantonly have destroyed or cast aside.

We mustn't allow ourselves to become the dupes of nostalgia. The best of the romantic theatre, the civilized pleasures of the opera and the ballet were in any event gross reductions of an art sacred in its origins. Over the centuries the Orphic Rites turned into the Gala Performance – slowly and imperceptibly the wine was adulterated drop by drop.

The curtain used to be the great symbol of a whole school of theatre – the red curtain, the footlights, the idea that we are all children again, the nostalgia and the magic were all of a piece. Gordon Craig spent his life railing against the theatre of illusion, but his most treasured memories were of painted trees and forests and his eyes would light up as he described effects of *trompe d'œil*. But the day came when the same red curtain no longer hid surprises, when we no longer wanted – or needed – to be children again, when the rough magic yielded to a harsher common-sense; then the curtain was pulled down and the footlights removed.

Certainly, we still wish to capture in our arts the invisible currents that rule our lives, but our vision is now locked to the dark end of the spectrum. Today the theatre of doubting, of unease, of trouble, of alarm, seems truer than the theatre with a noble aim. Even if the theatre had in its origins rituals that made the invisible incarnate, we must not forget that apart from certain Oriental theatres these rituals have been either lost or remain in seedy decay. Bach's vision has been scrupulously preserved by the accuracy of his notations: in Fra Angelico we witness true incarnation: but for us to attempt such processes today, where do we find the source? In Coventry, for instance, a new cathedral has been built, according to the best recipe for achieving a noble result. Honest, sincere artists, the 'best', have been grouped together to make a civilized stab at celebrating God and Man and Culture and Life through a collective act. So there is a new building, fine ideas, beautiful glass-work – only the ritual is threadbare. Those Ancient and Modern hymns, charming perhaps in a little country church, those numbers on the wall, those dog-collars and the lessons – they are sadly inadequate here. The new place cries out for a new ceremony, but of course it is the new ceremony that should have come first – it is the ceremony in all its meanings that should have dictated the shape of the place, as it did when all the great mosques and cathedrals and temples were built. Goodwill, sincerity, reverence, belief in culture are not quite enough: the outer form can only take on real authority if the ceremony has equal authority – and who today can possibly call the tune? Of course, today as at all times, we need to stage true rituals, but for rituals that could make theatre-going an experience that feeds our lives, true forms are needed. These are not at our disposal, and conferences and resolutions will not bring them our way.

The actor searches vainly for the sound of a vanished tradition, and critic and audience follow suit. We have lost all sense of ritual and ceremony – whether it be connected with Christmas, birthdays or funerals – but the words remain with us and old impulses stir in the marrow. We feel we should have rituals, we should do 'something' about getting them and we blame the artists for not 'finding' them for us. So the artist sometimes attempts to find new rituals with only his imagination as his source: he imitates the outer form of ceremonies, pagan or baroque, unfortunately adding his own trappings – the result is rarely convincing. And after the years and years of weaker and waterier imitations we now find ourselves rejecting the very notion of a holy stage. It is not the fault of the holy that it has become a middle-class weapon to keep children good.

When I first went to Stratford in 1945 every conceivable value was buried in deadly sentimentality and complacent worthiness – a traditionalism approved largely by town, scholar and press. It needed the boldness of a very extraordinary old gentleman, Sir Barry Jackson, to throw all this out of the window and so make a true search for true values possible once more. And it was at Stratford years later, at the official luncheon to celebrate Shakespeare's 400th birthday, that I saw a clear example of the difference between what a ritual is and what it could be. It was felt that Shakespeare's birthday called for a ritual celebration. The only celebration anyone could vaguely remember was related to a feast: and a feast today means a list of people from *Who's Who*, assembled round Prince Philip, eating smoked salmon and steak. Ambassadors nodded to one another and passed the ritual red wine. I chatted with the local M.P. Then someone made a formal speech, we listened politely – and rose to our feet to toast William Shakespeare. At the moment the glasses clinked – for not more than a fraction of a second, through the common consciousness of everyone present and all for once concentrating on the same thing – passed the notion that four hundred years ago such a man had been, and that this was what we were assembled for. For a breath of time the silence deepened, a touch of meaning was there – an instant later it was brushed away and forgotten. If we understood more about rituals, the ritual celebration of an individual to whom we owe so much might have been intentional, not accidental. It might have been as powerful as all his plays, and as un-forgettable. However, we do not know how to celebrate, because we do not know what to celebrate. All we know is the end result: we know and we like the feel and sound of cele-brating through applause, and this is where we get stuck. We forget that there are two possible climaxes to a theatre ex-perience. There is the climax of celebration in which our participation explodes in stamping and cheering, shouts of hurrah and the roar of hands, or else, at the other end of the stick, the climax of silence – another form of recognition and appreciation for an experience shared. We have largely for-gotten silence. It even embarrasses us; we clap our hands mechanically because we do not know what else to do, and we are unaware that silence is also permitted, that silence also is good.

It is only when a ritual comes to our own level that we become qualified to deal in it: the whole of pop music is a series of rituals on a level to which we have access. Peter Hall's vast and rich achievement in his cycle of Shakespeare's 'Wars of the Roses' drew on assassination, politics, intrigue, war: David Rudkin's disturbing play *Afore Night Come* was a ritual of death: *West Side Story* a ritual of urban violence, Genet creates rituals of sterility and degradation. When I took a tour of *Titus Andronicus* through Europe this obscure work of Shakespeare touched audiences directly because we had tapped in it a ritual of bloodshed which was recognized as true. And this leads to the heart of the controversy that exploded in London about what were labelled 'dirty plays': the complaint was that the theatre today is wallowing in misery; that in Shakespeare, in great classical art, one eye is always on the stars, that the rite of winter includes a sense of the rite of spring. I think this is true. In a sense I agree wholeheartedly with our opponents – but not when I see what they propose. They are not searching for a holy theatre, they are not talking about a theatre of miracles: they are talking of the tame play where 'higher' only means 'nicer' – being noble only means being decent – alas, happy endings and optimism can't be ordered like wine from cellars. They spring whether we wish it or not from a source and if we pretend there is such a source readily at hand we will go on cheating ourselves with rotten imitations. If we recognize how desperately far we have drifted from anything to do with a holy theatre we can begin to discard once and for all the dream that a fine theatre could return in a trice if only a few nice people tried harder.

More than ever, we crave for an experience that is beyond the humdrum. Some look for it in jazz, classical music, in marijuana and in LSD. In the theatre we shy away from the holy because we don't know what this could be – we only know that what is called the holy has let us down, we shrink from what is called poetic because the poetic has let us down. Attempts to revive poetic drama too often have led to something wishy-washy or obscure. Poetry has become a meaningless term, and its association with word-music, with sweet sounds, is a hangover of a Tennysonian tradition that has somehow wrapped itself round Shakespeare, so that we are conditioned by the idea that a verse play is half-way between prose and the opera, neither spoken nor sung, yet with a higher charge than prose – higher in content, higher somehow in moral value.

All the forms of sacred art have certainly been destroyed by bourgeois values but this sort of observation does not help our problem. It is foolish to allow a revulsion from bourgeois forms to turn into a revulsion from needs that are common to all men: if the need for a true contact with a sacred invisibility through the theatre still exists, then all possible vehicles must be re-examined.

I have sometimes been accused of wanting to destroy the spoken word, and indeed in this absurdity there's a grain of sense. In its fusion with the American idiom our ever-changing language has rarely been richer, and yet it does not seem that the word is the same tool for dramatists that it once was. Is it that we are living in an age of images? Is it even that we must go through a period of image-saturation, for the need for language to re-emerge? This is very possible, for today writers seem unable to make ideas and images collide through words with Elizabethan force. The most influential of modern writers, Brecht, wrote full and rich texts, but the real conviction of his plays is inseparable from the imagery of his own productions. Yet in the desert one prophet raised his voice. Railing against the sterility of the theatre before the war in France an illuminated genius, Antoine Artaud, wrote tracts describing from his imagination and intuition another theatre – a Holy Theatre in which the blazing centre speaks through those forms closest to it. A theatre working like the plague, by intoxication, by infection, by analogy, by magic; a theatre in which the play, the event itself, stands in place of a text.

Is there another language, just as exacting for the author, as a language of words? Is there a language of actions, a language of sounds – a language of word-as-part-of movement, of word-as-lie, word-as-parody, of word-as-rubbish, of word-as-contradiction, of word-shock or word-cry? If we talk of the more-than-literal, if poetry means that which crams more and penetrates deeper – is this where it lies? Charles Marowitz and I instituted a group with the Royal Shakespeare Theatre called the Theatre of Cruelty to investigate these questions and to try to learn for ourselves what a holy theatre might be.

The title was by way of homage to Artaud, but it did not mean that we were trying to reconstruct Artaud's own theatre. Anyone who wishes to know what 'Theatre of Cruelty' means should refer directly to Artaud's own writings. We used his striking title to cover our own experiments, many of which were directly stimulated by Artaud's thought – although many exercises were very far from what he had proposed. We did not start at the blazing centre, we began very simply on the fringes.

We set an actor in front of us, asked him to imagine a dramatic situation that did not involve any physical movement, then we all tried to understand what state he was in. Of course, this was impossible, which was the point of the exercise. The next stage was to discover what was the very least he needed before understanding could be reached: was it a sound, a movement, a rhythm – and were these inter-changeable – or had each its special strengths and limita-tions? So we worked by imposing drastic conditions. An actor must communicate an idea – the start must always be a thought or a wish that he has to project – but he has only, say, one finger, one tone of voice, a cry, or the capacity to whistle at his disposal.

An actor sits at one end of the room, facing the wall. At the other end another actor, looking at the first one's back, not allowed to move. The second actor must make the first one obey him. As the first one has his back turned, the second has no way of communicating his wishes except through sounds, for he is allowed no words. This seems impossible, but it can be done. It is like crossing an abyss on a tightrope: necessity suddenly produces strange powers. I have heard of a woman lifting a huge car off her injured child – a feat techni-cally impossible for her muscles in any predictable condi-tions. Ludmilla Pitoeff used to go on stage with her heart pounding in a way that in theory should have killed her every night. With this exercise, many times we also observed an equally phenomenal result: a long silence, great concentra-tion, one actor running experimentally through a range of hisses or gurgles until suddenly the other actor stood and quite confidently executed the movement the first one had in mind.

Similarly these actors experimented in communication through tapping with a finger-nail: starting from a powerful need to express something and again using only one tool. Here it was rhythm – on another occasion, it was the eyes or the back of the head. A valuable exercise was to fight in partners, taking and giving back every blow, but never being allowed to touch, never moving the head, nor the arms, nor feet. In other words a movement of the torso is all that is allowed: no realistic contact can take place, yet a fight must be engaged physically, emotionally and carried through. Such exercises should not be thought of as gymnastics – freeing muscular resistance is only a by-product – the purpose all

the time is to increase resistance – by limiting the alter-
natives – and then using this resistance in the struggle for a
true expression. The principle is the one of rubbing two
sticks together. This friction of unyielding opposites makes
fire – and other forms of combustion can be obtained in the
same way. The actor then found that to communicate his invisible meanings he needed concentration, he needed will; he
needed to summon all his emotional reserves; he needed
courage; he needed clear thought. But the most important
result was that he was led inexorably to the conclusion that he
needed form. It was not enough to feel passionately – a
creative leap was required to mint a new form which could
be a container and a reflector for his impulses. That is what
is truly called an 'action'. One of the most interesting
moments was during an exercise in which each member of the
group had to act a child. Naturally, one after the other did an
'imitation' of a child by stooping, wiggling, or squawking –
and the result was painfully embarrassing. Then the tallest
of the group came forward and without any physical change
at all, with no attempt to imitate baby talk, he presented fully
to everyone's complete satisfaction the idea that he had been
called upon to carry. How? I can't describe it; it happened as
direct communication, only for those present. This is what
some theatres call magic, others science, but it's the same
thing. An invisible idea was rightly shown.

I say 'shown' because an actor making a gesture is both
creating for himself out of his deepest need and yet for the
other person. It is hard to understand the true notion of
spectator, there and not there, ignored and yet needed. The
actor's work is never for an audience, yet always is for one.
The onlooker is a partner who must be forgotten and still
constantly kept in mind: a gesture is statement, expression,
communication and a private manifestation of loneliness – it
is always what Artaud calls a signal through the flames – yet
this implies a sharing of experience, once contact is made.

Slowly we worked towards different wordless languages:
we took an event, a fragment of experience and made exercises that turned them into forms that could be shared. We

encouraged the actors to see themselves not only as impro-
visers, lending themselves blindly to their inner impulses, but
as artists responsible for searching and selecting amongst
form, so that a gesture or a cry becomes like an object that he
discovers and even remoulds. We experimented with and
came to reject the traditional language of masks and make-
ups as no longer appropriate. We experimented with silence.
We set out to discover the relations between silence and
duration: we needed an audience so that we could set a silent
actor in front of them to see the varying lengths of attention
he could command. Then we experimented with ritual in the
sense of repetitive patterns, seeing how it is possible to present more meaning, more swiftly than by a logical unfolding
of events. Our aim for each experiment, good or bad, successful or disastrous, was the same: can the invisible be made
visible through the performer's presence?

We know that the world of appearance is a crust – under
the crust is the boiling matter we see if we peer into a vol-
cano. How can we tap this energy? We studied Meyerhold's
bio-mechanical experiments, where he played love scenes on
swings and in one of our performances a Hamlet threw
Ophelia on to the knees of the audience, while he swung
above their heads on a rope. We were denying psychology,
we were trying to smash the apparently water-tight divisions
between the private and the public man: the outer man whose
behaviour is bound by the photographic rules of everyday
life, who must sit to sit, stand to stand – and the inner man
whose anarchy and poetry is usually expressed only in his
words. For centuries, unrealistic speech has been universally
accepted, all sorts of audiences have swallowed the convention that words can do the strangest things – in a monologue,
for instance, a man stays still but his ideas can dance where
they will. Vaulting speech is a good convention, but is there
another? When a man flies over the audience's head on a
rope, every aspect of the immediate is put in jeopardy – the
circle of spectators that is at ease when the man speaks is
thrown into chaos: in this instant of hazard can a different
meaning appear?

In naturalistic plays the playwright contrives the dialogue in such a way that while seeming natural it shows what he wants to be seen. By using language illogically, by introducing the ridiculous in speech and the fantastic in behaviour, an author of the Theatre of the Absurd opens up for himself another vocabulary. For instance, a tiger comes into the room, but the couple take no notice: the wife speaks, the husband answers by taking off his pants and a new pair floats in through the window. The theatre of the Absurd did not seek the unreal for its own sake. It used the unreal to make certain explorations, because it sensed the absence of truth in our everyday exchanges, and the presence of the truth in the seeming far-fetched. Although there have been some remarkable individual works stemming from this approach to the world, as a recognizable school the Absurd has reached an impasse. Like so much that is novel in texture, like much concrete music, for instance, the surprise element wears thin, and we are left to face the fact that the field it covers is sometimes very small. Fantasy invented by the mind is apt to be lightweight, the whimsicality and the surrealism of much of the Absurd would no more have satisfied Artaud than the narrowness of the psychological play. What he wanted in his search for a holiness was absolute: he wanted a theatre that would be a hallowed place: he wanted that theatre served by a band of dedicated actors and directors who would create out of their own natures an unending succession of violent stage images, bringing about such powerful immediate explosions of human matter that no one would ever again revert to a theatre of anecdote and talk. He wanted the theatre to contain all that normally is reserved for crime and war. He wanted an audience that would drop all its defences, that would allow itself to be perforated, shocked, startled, and raped, so that at the same time it could be filled with a powerful new charge.

This sounds tremendous, yet it raises a nagging doubt. How passive does this make the spectator? Artaud maintained that only in the theatre could we liberate ourselves from the recognizable forms in which we live our daily lives.

This made the theatre a holy place in which a greater reality could be found. Those who view his work with suspicion ask how all-embracing is this truth, and secondly, how valuable is the experience? A totem, a cry from the womb: these can crack through walls of prejudice in any man: a howl can certainly reach through to the guts. But is this revealing, is this contact with our own repressions creative, therapeutic? Is it really holy – or is Artaud in his passion dragging us back to a nether world, away from striving, away from the light – to D. H. Lawrence, Wagner; is there even a fascist smell in the cult of unreason? Is a cult of the invisible, anti-intelligent? Is it a denial of the mind?

As with all prophets, we must separate the man from his followers. Artaud never attained his own theatre, maybe the power of his vision is that it is the carrot in front of our nose, never to be reached. Certainly, he himself was always speaking of a complete way of life, of a theatre in which the activity of the actor and the activity of the spectator are driven by the same desperate need.

Artaud applied is Artaud betrayed: betrayed because it is always just a portion of his thought that is exploited, betrayed because it is easier to apply rules to the work of a handful of dedicated actors than to the lives of the unknown spectators who happened by chance to come through the theatre door.

None the less, from the arresting words 'Theatre of Cruelty' comes a groping towards a theatre, more violent, less rational, more extreme, less verbal, more dangerous. There is a joy in violent shocks: the only trouble with violent shocks is that they wear off. What follows a shock? Here's the snag. I fire a pistol at the spectator – I did so once – and for a second I have a possibility to reach him in a different way. I must relate this possibility to a purpose, otherwise a moment later he is back where he was: inertia is the greatest force we know. I show a sheet of blue – nothing but the colour blue – blueness is a direct statement that arouses an emotion, the next second that impression fades: I hold up a brilliant flash of scarlet – a different impression is made, but unless someone can grab this moment, knowing why and how and what for – it too begins to wane. The trouble is that one can easily find oneself firing the first shots without any sense of where the battle could lead. One look at the average audience gives us an irresistible urge to assault it – to shoot first and ask questions later. This is the road to the Happening.

A Happening is a powerful invention, it destroys at one blow many deadly forms, like the dreariness of theatre buildings, and the charmless trappings of curtain, usherette, cloakroom, programme, bar. A Happening can be anywhere, any time, of any duration: nothing is required, nothing is taboo. A Happening may be spontaneous, it may be formal, it may be anarchistic, it can generate intoxicating energy. Behind the Happening is the shout 'Wake up!' Van Gogh made generations of travellers see Provence with new eyes, and the theory of Happenings is that a spectator can be jolted eventually into new sight, so that he wakes to the life around him. This sounds like sense, and in Happenings, the influence of Zen and Pop Art combine to make a perfectly logical twentieth-century American combination. But the sadness of a bad Happening must be seen to be believed. Give a child a paintbox, and if he mixes all the colours together the result is always the same muddy browny grey. A Happening is always the brainchild of someone and unavoidably it reflects the level of its inventor: if it is the work of a group, it reflects the inner resources of the group. This free form is all too often imprisoned in the same obsessional symbols; flour, custard pies, rolls of paper, dressing, undressing, dressing-up, undressing again, changing clothes, making water, throwing water, blowing water, hugging, rolling, writhing – you feel that if a Happening became a way of life then by contrast the most humdrum life would seem a fantastic happening. Very easily a Happening can be no more than a series of mild shocks followed by let-downs which progressively combine to neutralize the further shocks before they arrive. Or else the frenzy of the shocker bludgeons the shockee into becoming still another form of the Deadly Audience – he starts willing and is assaulted into apathy.

The simple fact is that Happenings have brought into being

not the easiest but the most exacting forms of all. As shocks and surprises make a dent in a spectator's reflexes, so that he is suddenly more open, more alert, more awake, the possibility and the responsibility arise for onlooker and performer alike. The instant must be used, but how, what for? Here, we are back to the root question – what are we searching for anyway? Do-it-yourself Zen hardly fits the bill. The Happening is a new broom of great efficacity: it is certainly sweeping away the rubbish, but as it clears the way the old dialogue is heard again, the debate of form against formless, freedom against discipline; a dialectic as old as Pythagoras, who first set in opposition the terms Limit and Unlimited. It is all very well to use crumbs of Zen to assert the principle that existence is existence, that every manifestation contains within it all of everything, and that a slap on the face, a tweak of the nose or a custard pie are all equally Buddha. All religions assert that the invisible is visible all the time. But here's the crunch. Religious teaching – including Zen – asserts that this visible-invisible cannot be seen automatically – it can only be seen given certain conditions. The conditions can relate to certain states or to a certain understanding. In any event, to comprehend the visibility of the invisible is a life's work. Holy art is an aid to this, and so we arrive at a definition of a holy theatre. A holy theatre not only presents the invisible but also offers conditions that make its perception possible. The Happening could be related to all of this, but the present inadequacy of the Happening is that it refuses to examine deeply the problem of perception. Naïvely it believes that the cry 'Wake up!' is enough: that the call 'Live!' brings life. Of course, more is needed. But what?

A happening was originally intended to be a painter's creation – which instead of paint and canvas, or glue and saw-dust, or solid objects, used people to make certain relationships and forms. Like a painting, a happening is intended as a new object, a new construction brought into the world, to enrich the world, to add to nature, to sit alongside everyday life. To those who find happenings dreary the supporter retorts that any one thing is as good as another. If some seem

'worse' than others, this, they say, is the result of the spectator's conditioning and his jaded eye. Those who take part
in a happening and get a kick out of doing so can afford to
regard the outsider's boredom with indifference. The very
fact that they participate heightens their perception. The man
who puts on a dinner jacket for the opera, saying, 'I enjoy a
sense of occasion', and the hippy who puts on a flowered suit
for an all-night light-show are both reaching incoherently in
the same direction. Occasion, Event, Happening – the words
are interchangeable. The structures are different – the opera is
constructed and repeated according to traditional principles,
the light-show unfolds for the first and last time according to
accident and environment; but both are deliberately constructed social gatherings that seek for an invisibility to inter-
penetrate and animate the ordinary. Those of us who work
in theatres are implicitly challenged to go ahead to meet this
hunger.

There are many people attempting in their own ways to
take up the challenge. I will quote three.

There is Merce Cunningham. Stemming from Martha
Graham, he has evolved a ballet company whose daily
exercises are a continual preparation for the shock of freedom. A classical dancer is trained to observe and follow
every detail of a movement that he is given. He has trained
his body to obey, his technique is his servant, so that instead
of being wrapped up in the doing of the movement he can let
the movement unfold in intimate company with the unfolding
of the music. Merce Cunningham's dancers, who are highly
trained, use their discipline to be more aware of the fine
currents that flow within a movement as it unfolds for the
first time – and their technique enables them to follow this
fine prompting, freed from the clumsiness of the untrained
man. When they improvise – as notions are born and flow
between them, never repeating themselves, always in movement – the intervals have shape, so that the rhythms can be
sensed as just and the proportions as true: all is spontaneous
and yet there is order. In silence there are many potentialities;
chaos or order, muddle or pattern, all lie fallow – the invisible

made visible is of a sacred nature, and as he dances Merce Cunningham strives for a holy art.

Perhaps the most intense and personal writing of our time comes from Samuel Beckett. Beckett's plays are symbols in an exact sense of the word. A false symbol is soft and vague: a true symbol is hard and clear. When we say 'symbolic' we often mean something drearily obscure: a true symbol is specific, it is the only form a certain truth can take. The two men waiting by a stunted tree, the man recording himself on tapes, the two men marooned in a tower, the woman buried to her waist in sand, the parents in the dustbins, the three heads in the urns: these are pure inventions, fresh images sharply defined – and they stand on the stage as objects. They are theatre machines. People smile at them, but they hold their ground: they are critic-proof. We get nowhere if we expect to be told what they mean, yet each one has a relation with us we can't deny. If we accept this, the symbol opens in us a great and wondering O.

This is how Beckett's dark plays are plays of light, where the desperate object created is witness of the ferocity of the wish to bear witness to the truth. Beckett does not say 'no' with satisfaction; he forges his merciless 'no' out of a longing for 'yes' and so his despair is the negative from which the contour of its opposite can be drawn.

There are two ways of speaking about the human condition: there is the process of inspiration – by which all the positive elements of life can be revealed, and there is the process of honest vision – by which the artist bears witness to whatever it is that he has seen. The first process depends on revelation; it can't be brought about by holy wishes. The second one depends on honesty, and it mustn't be clouded over by holy wishes.

Beckett expresses just this distinction in *Happy Days*. The optimism of the lady buried in the ground is not a virtue, it is the element that blinds her to the truth of her situation. For a few rare flashes she glimpses her condition, but at once she blots them out with her good cheer. Beckett's action on some of his audience is exactly like the action of this situation on the leading character. The audience wriggles, squirms and yawns, it walks out or else invents and prints every form of imaginary complaint as a mechanism to ward off the uncomfortable truth. Sadly, it is the wish for optimism that many writers share that prevents them from finding hope. When we attack Beckett for pessimism it is we who are the Beckett characters trapped in a Beckett scene. When we accept Beckett's statement as it is, then suddenly all is transformed. There is after all quite another audience, Beckett's audience; those in every country who do not set up intellectual barriers, who do not try too hard to analyse the message. This audience laughs and cries out – and in the end celebrates with Beckett; this audience leaves his plays, his black plays, nourished and enriched, with a lighter heart, full of a strange irrational joy. Poetry, nobility, beauty, magic – suddenly these suspect words are back in the theatre once more.

In Poland there is a small company led by a visionary, Jerzy Grotowski, that also has a sacred aim. The theatre, he believes, cannot be an end in itself; like dancing or music in certain dervish orders, the theatre is a vehicle, a means for self-study, self-exploration; a possibility of salvation. The actor has himself as his field of work. This field is richer than that of the painter, richer than that of the musician, because to explore he needs to call on every aspect of himself. His hand, his eye, his ear, and his heart are what he is studying and what he is studying with. Seen this way, acting is a life's work – the actor is step by step extending his knowledge of himself through the painful, everchanging circumstances of rehearsal and the tremendous punctuation points of performance. In Grotowski's terminology, the actor allows a role to 'penetrate' him; at first he is all obstacle to it, but by constant work he acquires technical mastery over his physical and psychic means by which he can allow the barriers to drop. 'Auto-penetration' by the role is related to exposure: the actor does not hesitate to show himself exactly as he is, for he realizes that the secret of the role demands his opening himself up, disclosing his own secrets. So that the act of performance is an act of sacrifice, of sacrificing what most men prefer to hide – this sacrifice is his gift to the spectator. Here there is a similar relation between actor and audience to the one between priest and worshipper. It is obvious that not everyone is called to priesthood and no traditional religion expects this of all men. There are laymen – who have necessary roles in life – and those who take on other burdens, for the laymen's sake. The priest performs the ritual for himself and on behalf of others. Grotowski's actors offer their performance as a ceremony for those who wish to assist: the actor invokes, lays bare what lies in every man – and what daily life covers up. This theatre is holy because its purpose is holy; it has a clearly defined place in the community and it responds to a need the churches can no longer fill. Grotowski's theatre is as close as anyone has got to Artaud's ideal. It is a complete way of life for all its members, and so it is in contrast with most other *avant-garde* and experimental groups whose work is scrambled and usually invalidated through lack of means. Most experimental products cannot do what they want because outside conditions are too heavily loaded against them. They have scratch casts, rehearsal time eaten into by the need to earn their living, inadequate sets, costumes, lights, etc. Poverty is their complaint and their excuse. Grotowski makes poverty an ideal; his actors have given up everything except their own bodies; they have the human instrument and limitless time – no wonder they feel the richest theatre in the world.

These three theatres, Cunningham, Grotowski, and Beckett have several things in common; small means, intense work, rigorous discipline, absolute precision. Also, almost as a condition, they are theatres for an *élite*. Merce Cunningham usually plays to poor houses, and if his admirers are scandalized by his lack of support he himself takes it in his stride. Beckett only rarely fills an average sized auditorium. Grotowski plays for thirty spectators – as a deliberate choice. He is convinced that the problems facing himself and the actor are so great that to consider a larger audience could only lead to a dilution of the work. He said to me: 'My search is based on the director and the actor. You base yours on the director, actor, audience. I accept that this is possible, but for me it is too indirect.' Is he right? Are these the only possible theatres to touch 'reality'? They are certainly true to themselves, they certainly face the basic question, 'Why theatre at all?' and each one has found its answer. They each start from their hunger, each works to lessen his own need. And yet the very purity of their resolve, the high and serious nature of their activity inevitably brings a colour to their choices and a limitation to their field. They are unable to be both esoteric and popular at one and the same time. There is no crowd in Beckett, no Falstaff. For Merce Cunningham, as once for Schoenberg, it would need a *tour de force* to re-invent Ring a ring o' Roses or to whistle *God Save The Queen*. In life, Grotowski's leading actor avidly collects jazz records, but there are no pop lyrics on the stage which is his life. These theatres explore life, yet what counts as life is restricted. 'Real' life precludes certain 'unreal' features. If we read today Artaud's descriptions of his imaginary productions, they reflect his own tastes and the current romantic imagery of his time, for there is a certain preference for darkness and mystery, for chanting, for unearthly cries, for single words rather than sentences, for vast shapes, masks, for kings and emperors and popes, for saints and sinners and flagellants, for black tights and writhing naked skin.

A director dealing with elements that exist outside of himself can cheat himself into thinking his work more objective than it is. By his choice of exercises, even by the way he encourages an actor to find his own freedom, a director cannot help projecting his own state of mind on to the stage. The supreme jujitsu would be for the director to stimulate such an outpouring of the actor's inner richness that it completely transforms the subjective nature of his original impulse. But usually the director or the choreographer's pattern shows through and it is here that the desired objective experience can turn into the expression of some individual director's private imagery. We can try to capture the invisible but we must not lose touch with common-sense – if our language is too special we will lose part of the spectator's belief. The

model, as always, is Shakespeare. His aim continually is
holy, metaphysical, yet he never makes the mistake of stay-
ing too long on the highest plane. He knew how hard it is
for us to keep company with the absolute – so he continually
bumps us down to earth – and Grotowski recognizes this,
speaking of the need for both 'apotheosis' and 'derision'. We
have to accept that we can never see all of the invisible. So
after straining towards it, we have to face defeat, drop down
to earth, then start up again.

I have refrained from introducing the Living Theatre until
now because this group, led by Julian Beck and Judith
Malina, is special in every sense of the word. It is a nomad
community. It moves across the world according to its own
laws and often in contradiction to the laws of the country in
which it happens to be. It provides a complete way of life
for every one of its members, some thirty men and women
who live and work together; they make love, produce children, act, invent plays, do physical and spiritual exercises,
share and discuss everything that comes their way. Above all,
they are a community; but they are only a community because they have a special function which gives their communal
existence its meaning. This function is acting. Without acting
the group would run dry: they perform because the act and
fact of performing corresponds to a great shared need. They
are in search of meaning in their lives, and in a sense even
if there were no audiences, they would still have to perform,
because the theatrical event is the climax and centre of their
search. Yet without an audience their performances would
lose their substance – the audience is always the challenge
without which a performance would be a sham. Also, it is a
practical community that makes performances for a living and
offers them for sale. In the Living Theatre, three needs become one: it exists for the sake of performing, it earns its
living through performing and its performances contain the
most intense and intimate moments of its collective life.

One day this caravan may halt. This could be in a hostile
environment – like its origins in New York – in which case
its function will be to provoke and divide audiences by in-

creasing their awareness of uncomfortable contradiction between a way of life on stage and a way of life outside. Their own identity will be constantly drawn and redrawn by the natural tension and hostility between themselves and their surroundings. Alternatively, they may come to rest in some wider community that shares some of their values. Here there would be a different unity and a different tension: the tension would be shared by stage and audience – it would be the expression of the unresolved quest for a holiness eternally undefined.

In fact, the Living Theatre, exemplary in so many ways, has still not yet come to grips with its own essential dilemma. Searching for holiness without tradition, without source, it is compelled to turn to many traditions, many sources – yoga, Zen, psychoanalysis, books, hearsay, discovery, inspiration – a rich but dangerous eclecticism. For the method that leads to what they are seeking cannot be an additive one. To subtract, to strip away can only be effected in the light of some constant. They are still in search of this constant.

In the meantime, they are continually nourished by a very American humour and joy that is surrealist, but with both feet firmly on the ground.

* * *

In Haitian voodoo, all you need to begin a ceremony is a pole and people. You begin to beat the drums and far away in Africa the gods hear your call. They decide to come to you, and as voodoo is a very practical religion, it takes into account the time that a god needs to cross the Atlantic. So you go on beating your drum, chanting and drinking rum. In this way, you prepare yourself. Then five or six hours pass and the gods fly in – they circle above your heads, but it is not worth looking up as naturally they are invisible. This is where the pole becomes so vital. Without the pole nothing can link the visible and the invisible worlds. The pole, like the cross, is the junction. Through the wood, earthed, the spirits slide, and now they are ready for the second step in their metamorphosis. Now they need a human vehicle, and they choose one of the participants. A kick, a moan or two, a short paroxysm on the ground and a man is possessed. He gets to his feet, no longer himself, but filled with the god. The god now has form. He is someone who can joke, get drunk and listen to everyone's complaints. The first thing that the priest, the Houngan, does when the god arrives is to shake him by the hand and ask him about his trip. He's a god all right, but he is no longer unreal: he is there, on our level, attainable. The ordinary man or woman now can talk to him, pump his hand, argue, curse him, go to bed with him – and so, nightly, the Haitian is in contact with the great powers and mysteries that rule his day.

In the theatre, the tendency for centuries has been to put the actor at a remote distance, on a platform, framed, decorated, lit, painted, in high shoes – so as to help to persuade the ignorant that he is holy, that his art is sacred. Did this express reverence? Or was there behind it a fear that something would be exposed if the light were too bright, the meeting too near? Today, we have exposed the sham. But we are rediscovering that a holy theatre is still what we need. So where should we look for it? In the clouds or on the ground?

3

The Rough Theatre

IT IS always the popular theatre that saves the day. Through the ages it has taken many forms, and there is only one factor that they all have in common – a roughness. Salt, sweat, noise, smell: the theatre that's not in a theatre, the theatre on carts, on wagons, on trestles, audiences standing, drinking, sitting round tables, audiences joining in, answering back: theatre in back rooms, upstairs rooms, barns; the one-night stands, the torn sheet pinned up across the hall, the battered screen to conceal the quick changes – that one generic term, *theatre*, covers all this and the sparkling chandeliers too. I have had many abortive discussions with architects building new theatres – trying vainly to find words with which to communicate my own conviction that it is not a question of good buildings and bad: a beautiful place may never bring about explosion of life; while a haphazard hall may be a tremendous meeting place: this is the mystery of the theatre, but in the understanding of this mystery lies the only possibility of ordering it into a science. In other forms of architecture there is a relationship between conscious, articulate design and good functioning: a well-designed hospital may be more efficacious than a higgledy-piggledy one; but as for theatres, the problem of design cannot start logically. It is not a matter of saying analytically what are the requirements, how best they can be organized – this will usually bring into existence a tame, conventional, often cold hall. The science of theatre-building must come from studying what it is that brings about the most vivid relationship between people – and is this best served by asymmetry, even by disorder? If so, what can be the rule of this disorder? An architect is better off if he works like a scene designer, moving scraps of cardboard by intuition, than if he builds his model from a plan, prepared with compass and ruler. If we find that dung is a good fertilizer, it is no use being squeamish; if the theatre seems to need a certain crude element, this must be accepted as part of its natural soil. At the beginning of electronic music, some German studios claimed that they could make every sound that a natural instrument could make – only better. They then discovered that all their sounds were marked by a certain uniform sterility. So they analysed the sounds made by clarinets, flutes, violins, and found that each note contained a remarkably high proportion of plain noise: actual scraping, or the mixture of heavy breathing with wind on wood: from a purist point of view this was just dirt, but the composers soon found themselves compelled to make synthetic dirt – to 'humanize' their compositions. Architects remain blind to this principle – and era after era the most vital theatrical experiences occur outside the legitimate places constructed for the purpose. Gordon Craig influenced Europe for half a century through a couple of performances given in Hampstead in a church hall – the signature of the Brecht theatre, the white half-curtain, originated quite practically in a cellar, when a wire had to be slung from wall to wall. The Rough Theatre is close to the people: it may be a puppet theatre, it may – as in Greek villages to this day – be a shadow show: it is usually distinguished by the absence of what is called style. Style needs leisure: putting over something in rough conditions is like a revolution, for anything that comes to hand can be turned into a weapon. The Rough Theatre doesn't pick and choose: if the audience is restive, then it is obviously more important to holler at the trouble makers – or improvise a gag – than to try to preserve the unity of style of the scene. In the luxury of the high-class theatre, everything can be all of a piece: in a rough theatre a bucket will be banged for a battle, flour used to show faces white with fear. The arsenal is limitless: the aside, the placard, the topical reference, the local jokes, the exploiting of accidents, the songs, the dances, the tempo, the noise, the relying on contrasts, the shorthand of exaggeration, the false noses, the stock types, the stuffed bellies. The popular theatre, freed of unity of style, actually speaks a very sophisticated and stylish language: a popular audience usually has no difficulty in accepting inconsistencies of accent and dress, or in darting between mime and dialogue, realism and suggestion. They follow the line of story, unaware in fact that somewhere there is a set of standards which are being broken. Martin Esslin has written that in San Quentin prisoners seeing a play for the first time in their lives and being confronted with *Waiting for Godot* had no problem at all in following what to regular theatregoers was incomprehensible.

One of the pioneer figures in the movement towards a renewed Shakespeare was William Poel. An actress once told me that she had worked with Poel in a production of *Much Ado About Nothing* that was presented some fifty years ago for one night in some gloomy London Hall. She said that at the first rehearsal Poel arrived with a case full of scraps out of which he brought odd photographs, drawings, pictures torn out of magazines. 'That's you,' he said, giving her a picture of a debutante at the Royal Garden Party. To someone else it was a knight in armour, a Gainsborough portrait or else just a hat. In all simplicity, he was expressing the way he saw the play when he read it – directly, as a child does – not as a grown-up monitoring himself with notions of history and period. My friend told me that the total pre-pop-art mixture had an extraordinary homogeneity. I am sure of it. Poel was a great innovator and he clearly saw that consistency had no relation to real Shakespearian style. I once did a production of *Love's Labour's Lost* where I dressed the character called Constable Dull as a Victorian policeman because his name at once conjured up the typical figure of the London bobby. For other reasons the rest of the characters were dressed in Watteau-eighteenth-century clothes, but no one was conscious of an anachronism. A long time ago I saw a production of *The Taming of the Shrew* where all the actors dressed themselves exactly the way they saw the characters – I still remember a cowboy, and a fat character busting the buttons of a pageboy's uniform – and that it was far and away the most satisfying rendering of this play I have seen.

Of course, it is most of all dirt that gives the roughness its edge; filth and vulgarity are natural, obscenity is joyous: with these the spectacle takes on its socially liberating role, for by nature the popular theatre is anti-authoritarian, anti-traditional, anti-pomp, anti-pretence. This is the theatre of noise, and the theatre of noise is the theatre of applause.

Think of those two awful masks that glower at us from so many books on theatre – in ancient Greece we are told these masks represented two equal elements, tragedy and comedy. At least, they are always shown as equal partners. Since then, though, the 'legitimate' theatre has been considered the important one while the Rough Theatre has been thought less serious. But every attempt to revitalize the theatre has gone back to the popular source. Meyerhold had the highest aims, he sought to present all of life on the stage, his revered master was Stanislavsky, his friend was Chekhov; but in fact it was to the circus and the music hall that he turned. Brecht was rooted in the cabaret: Joan Littlewood longs for a fun-fair: Cocteau, Artaud, Vakhtangov, the most improbable bedfellows, all these highbrows return to the people: and Total Theatre is just a mix-up of these ingredients. All the time, experimental theatre comes out of the theatre buildings and returns to the room or the ring: it is the American musi-cal on the rare occasions when it fulfils its promise, and not the opera, that is the real meeting place of the American arts. It is to Broadway that American poets, choreographers and composers turn. A choreographer like Jerome Robbins is an interesting example, moving from the pure and abstract theatres of Balanchine and Martha Graham towards the roughness of the popular show. But the word 'popular' doesn't quite fill the bill: 'popular' conjures up the country fair and the people in a jolly harmless way. The popular tradition is also bearbaiting, ferocious satire and grotesque caricature. This quality was present in the greatest of rough theatres, the Elizabethan one, and in the English theatre today obscenity and truculence have become the motors of revival. Surrealism is rough – Jarry is rough. Spike Milligan's theatre, in which the imagination, freed by anarchy, flies like a wild bat in and out of every possible shape and style, has it all. Milligan, Charles Wood and a few others are a pointer towards what may become a powerful English tradition.

I saw two productions of Jarry's *Ubi Roi* which illustrated the difference between a rough and an artistic tradition. There was a production of *Ubu* on French television that by electronic means pulled off a great feat of virtuosity. The director very brilliantly succeeded in capturing with live actors the impression of black and white marionettes: the screen was subdivided into narrow bands so that it looked like a comic strip. M. Ubu and Mme Ubu were Jarry's drawings animated – they were Ubu to the letter. But not to the life; the television audience never accepted the crude reality of the story: it saw some pirouetting dolls, got baffled and bored and soon switched off. The virulent protest play had become a high-brow *jeu d'esprit*. At about the same time, on German television there was a Czech production of *Ubu*. This version disregarded every one of Jarry's images and indications: it invented an up-to-the-minute pop-art style of its own, made out of dustbins, garbage and ancient iron bedsteads: M. Ubu was no masked Humpty-Dumpty but a recognizable and shifty slob – Mme Ubu was a sleazy, attractive whore, the social context clear. From the first shot of M. Ubu stumbling in his underpants out of bed while a nagging voice from the pillows asked why he wasn't King of Poland, the audience's belief was caught and it could follow the surrealist developments of the story because it accepted the primitive situation and characters on their own terms.

This all concerns the appearance of roughness, but what is this theatre's intent? First of all it is there unashamedly to make joy and laughter, what Tyrone Guthrie calls 'theatre of delight' and any theatre that can truly give delight has earned its place. Along with serious, committed and probing work, there must be irresponsibility. This is what the commercial theatre, the boulevard theatre, can give us – but all too often it is tired and threadbare. Fun continually needs a new electric charge: fun for fun's sake is not impossible, but seldom enough. Frivolity can be its charge: high spirits can make a good current, but all the time the batteries have to be replenished: new faces, new ideas have to be found. A new joke flashes and is gone; then it is the old joke that returns. The strongest comedy is rooted in archetypes, in mythology in basic recurrent situations; and inevitably it is deeply embedded in the social tradition. Comedy does not always stem from the main flow of a social argument: it is as though different comic traditions branch away in many directions: for a certain time, although the course is out of sight, the stream continues to flow on, then one day, unexpectedly, it dries up completely.

There is no hard and fast rule to say that one must never just cultivate effects and surfaces for their own sake. Why not? Personally, I find staging a musical can be more thoroughly enjoyable than any other form of theatre. Cultivating a deft sleight of hand can give one great delight. But an impression of freshness is everything – preserved foods lose their taste. The Holy Theatre has one energy, the Rough has others. Lightheartedness and gaiety feeds it, but so does the same energy that produces rebellion and opposition. This is a militant energy: it is the energy of anger, sometimes the energy of hate. The creative energy behind the richness of invention in the Berliner Ensemble's production of *The Days of the Commune* is the same energy that could man the barricades: the energy of *Arturo Ui* could go straight to war. The wish to change society, to get it to confront its eternal hypocrisies, is a great powerhouse. Figaro or Falstaff or Tartuffe lampoon and debunk through laughter, and the author's purpose is to bring about a social change.

John Arden's remarkable play *Sergeant Musgrave's Dance* can be taken amongst many other meanings as an illustration of how true theatre comes into being. Musgrave faces a crowd in a market place on an improvised stage and he attempts to communicate as forcibly as possible his sense of the horror and futility of war. The demonstration that he improvises is like a genuine piece of popular theatre, his props are machine-guns, flags, and a uniformed skeleton that he hauls aloft. When this does not succeed in transmitting his complete message to the crowd, his desperate energy drives him to find still further means of expression and in a flash of inspiration he begins a rhythmic stamp, out of which develops a savage dance and chant. Sergeant Musgrave's dance is a demonstration of how a violent need to project a meaning can suddenly call into existence a wild unpredictable form.

Here we see the double aspect of the rough: if the holy is the yearning for the invisible through its visible incarnations, the rough also is a dynamic stab at a certain ideal. Both theatres feed on deep and true aspirations in their audiences, both tap infinite resources of energy, of different energies: but both end by setting up areas in which certain things just aren't admitted. If the holy makes a world in which a prayer is more real than a belch, in the rough theatre, it is the other way round. The belching then, is real and prayer would be considered comic. The Rough Theatre has apparently no style, no conventions, no limitations – in practice, it has all three. Just as in life the wearing of old clothes can start as defiance and turn into a posture, so roughness can become an end in itself. The defiant popular theatre man can be so down-to-earth that he forbids his material to fly. He can even deny flight as a possibility, or the heavens as a suitable place to wander. This brings us to the point where the Holy Theatre and the Rough Theatre show their true antagonism to one another. The Holy Theatre deals with the invisible and this invisible contains all the hidden impulses of man. The Rough Theatre deals with men's actions, and because it is down to earth and direct – because it admits wickedness and laughter – the rough and ready seems better than the hollowly holy.

It is impossible to consider this further without stopping to look at the implications of the strongest, most influential and the most radical theatre man of our time, Brecht. No one seriously concerned with the theatre can by-pass Brecht.

Brecht is the key figure of our time, and all theatre work to-day at some point starts or returns to his statements and achievement. We can turn directly to the word that he brought into our vocabulary – alienation. As coiner of the term *alienation*, Brecht must be considered historically. He began working at a time when most German stages were dominated either by naturalism or by great total-theatre onslaughts of an operatic nature designed to sweep up the spectator by his emotions so that he forgot himself completely. Whatever life there was on-stage was offset by the passivity it demanded of the audience.

For Brecht, a necessary theatre could never for one moment take its sights off the society it was serving. There was no fourth wall between actors and audience – the actor's unique aim was to create a precise response in an audience for whom he had total respect. It was out of respect for the audience that Brecht introduced the idea of alienation, for alienation is a call to halt: alienation is cutting, interrupting, holding something up to the light, making us look again. Alienation is above all an appeal to the spectator to work for himself, so to become more and more responsible for accepting what he sees only if it is convincing to him in an adult way. Brecht rejects the romantic notion that in the theatre we all become children again.

The alienation effect and the happening effect are similar and opposite – the happening shock is there to smash through all the barriers set up by our reason, alienation is to shock us into bringing the best of our reason into play. Alienation works in many ways on many keys. A normal stage action will appear real to us if it is convincing and so we are apt to take it, temporarily, as objective truth. A girl, raped, walks on to a stage in tears – and if her acting touches us sufficiently, we automatically accept the implied conclusion that she is a victim and an unfortunate one. But suppose a clown were to follow her, mimicking her tears, and suppose by his talent he succeeds in making us laugh. His mockery destroys our first response. Then where do our sympathies go? The truth of her character, the validity of her position, are both put into question by the clown, and at the same time our own easy sentimentality is exposed. If carried far enough, such a series of events can suddenly make us confront our shifting views of right and wrong. All this stems from a strict sense of purpose. Brecht believed that, in making an audience take stock of the elements in a situation, the theatre was serving the purpose of leading its audience to a juster understanding of the society in which it lived, and so to learning in what ways that society was capable of change.

Alienation can work through antithesis; parody, imitation, criticism, the whole range of rhetoric is open to it. It is the purely theatrical method of dialectical exchange. Alienation is the language open to us today that is as rich in potentiality as verse: it is the possible device of a dynamic theatre in a changing world, and through alienation we could reach some of those areas that Shakespeare touched by his use of dynamic devices in language. Alienation can be very simple, it can be no more than a set of physical tricks. The first alienation device I ever saw was as a child, in a Swedish church; the collection bag had a spike on the end of it to nudge those of the congregation whom the sermon had sent to sleep. Brecht used placards and visible spotlights for the same purpose; Joan Littlewood dressed her soldiers as Pierrots – alienation has endless possibilities. It aims continually at pricking the balloons of rhetorical playing – Chaplin's contrasting senti-mentality and calamity is alienation. Often when an actor is carried away by his part he can get more and more exaggerated, more and more cheaply emotional, and yet sweep the audience along with him. Here the alienating device will keep us awake when part of us wishes to surrender wholly to the tug on the heartstrings. But it is very hard to interfere with a spectator's stock reactions. At the end of the first act of *Lear* when Gloucester is blinded, we brought the house lights up before the last savage action was completed – so as to make the audience take stock of the scene before being engulfed in automatic applause. In Paris, with *The Representative* we again did all in our power to inhibit applause, because appreciation of the actor's talents seemed irrelevant in a Concentration Camp document. None the less, both the unfortunate Gloucester and the most nauseating character of all, the Auschwitz doctor, always left the stage to similar rounds of applause.

Jean Genet can write the most eloquent language, but the amazing impressions in his plays are very often brought about by the visual inventions with which he juxtaposes serious, beautiful, grotesque and ridiculous elements. There are few things in the modern theatre as compact and spellbinding as the climax of the first portion of *The Screens* when the stage action is a scribbling graffiti of war on to vast white surfaces, while violent phrases, ludicrous people and outsize dummies all together form a monument to colonialism and revolution. Here the potency of the conception is inseparable from the multi-levelled series of devices that become its expression. Genet's *The Blacks* takes on its full meaning when there is a powerful shifting relationship between actors and public. In Paris, witnessed by intellectuals, the play was baroque literary entertainment; in London, where no audience could be found who cared about either French literature or Negroes, the play was meaningless; in New York, in Gene Frankel's superb production it was electric and vibrant. I am told the vibrations changed from night to night depending on the proportion of blacks to whites in the house.

The *Marat/Sade* could not have existed before Brecht: it is conceived by Peter Weiss on many alienating levels: the events of the French Revolution cannot be accepted literally because they are being played by madmen, and their actions in turn are open to further question because their director is the Marquis de Sade – and moreover the events of 1780 are being seen with the eyes both of 1808 and of 1966 – for the people watching the play represent an early nineteenth-century audience and yet are also their twentieth-century selves. All these criss-crossing planes thicken the reference at each moment and compel an activity from each member of the public. At the end of the play the asylum goes berserk: all the actors improvise with the utmost violence and for an instant the stage image is naturalistic and compelling. Nothing, we feel, could ever stop this riot: nothing, we conclude, can ever stop the madness of the world. Yet it was at this moment, in the Royal Shakespeare Theatre version, that a stage manageress walked on to the stage, blew a whistle, and the madness immediately ended. In this action, a conundrum was presented. A second ago, the situation had been hopeless: now it is all over, the actors are pulling off their wigs: of course, it's just a play. So we begin to applaud. But unexpectedly the actors applaud us back, ironically. We react to this by a momentary hostility against them as individuals, and we stop clapping. I quote this as a typical alienation series, of which each incident forces us to readjust our position.

There is an interesting relationship between Brecht and Craig – Craig wanted a token shadow to take the place of a complete painted forest and he only did so because he recognised that useless information absorbed our attention *at the expense of something more important*. Brecht took this rigour and applied it not only to scenery but to the work of the actor and to the attitude of the audience. If he cut out superfluous emotion, and the development of characteristics and feelings that related only to the character, it was because he saw that the clarity of his theme was threatened. An actor in other German theatres of Brecht's day – and many an English actor today – believes that his entire job is to present his character as fully as possible, in the round. This means that he spends his observation and his imagination in finding additional details for his portrait, for, like the society painter, he wants the picture to be as life-like and recognizable as possible. No one has told him there could be any other aim. Brecht introduced the simple and devastating idea that 'fully' need not mean 'lifelike' nor 'in the round'. He pointed out that every actor has to serve the action of the play, but until the actor understands what the true action of the play is, what its true purpose is, from the author's point of view and in relation to the needs of a changing world outside (and what side is he himself on in the struggles that divide the world), he cannot possibly know what he is serving. However, when he understands precisely what is demanded of him, what he must fulfil, then he can properly understand his role. When he sees himself in relation to the wholeness of the play he will see that not only is too much characterizing often opposed to the play's needs but also that many unnecessary characteristics can actually work against him and make his own appearance less striking. He will then see the character he is playing more impartially, he will look at its sympathetic or unsympathetic features from a different viewpoint, and in the end will make different decisions from those he made when he thought 'identifying' with the character was all that mattered. Of course, this is a theory that can easily muddle an actor, because if he attempts to implement it naïvely by squashing his instincts and becoming an intellectual, he will end in disaster. It is a mistake to think that any actor can do work by theory alone. No actor can play a cipher: however stylized or schematic the writing, the actor *must* always believe to some degree in the stage life of the odd animal he represents. But none the less an actor can play in a thousand ways, and playing a portrait is not the only alternative. What Brecht introduced was the idea of the intelligent actor, capable of judging the value of his contribution. There were and still are many actors who pride themselves on knowing nothing about politics and who treat the theatre as an ivory tower. For Brecht such an actor is not worthy of his place in adult company: an actor in a community that supports a theatre must be as much involved in the outside world as in his own craft.

When theory is put into words, the door is opened to confusion. Brecht productions outside the Berliner Ensemble that are based on Brecht's essays have had Brecht economy, but rarely his richness of thought and feeling. These are often shunned, and so the work appears dry. The liveliest of theatres turns deadly when its coarse vigour goes: and Brecht is destroyed by deadly slaves. When Brecht talks of actors understanding their function, he never imagined that all could be achieved by analysis and discussion. The theatre is not the classroom, and a director with a pedagogic understanding of Brecht can no more animate his plays than a pedant those of Shakespeare. The quality of the work done in any rehearsal comes entirely from the creativity of the working climate – and creativity cannot be brought into being by explanations. The language of rehearsals is like life itself: it uses words, but also silences, stimuli, parody, laughter, unhappiness, despair, frankness and concealment, activity and slowness, clarity and chaos. Brecht recognized this and in his last years he surprised his associates by saying that the theatre must be naïve. With this word he was not reneging his life's work: he was pointing out that the action of putting together a play is always a form of playing, that watching a play is playing: he spoke disconcertingly of elegance and of entertainment. It is not by chance that in many languages the word for a play and to play is the same.

In his theoretical writing Brecht separates the real from the unreal, and I believe that this has been the source of a giant confusion. In terms of semantics the subjective is always opposed to the objective, the illusion separated from the fact. Because of these, his theatre is forced to maintain two positions: public and private, official and unofficial, theoretical and practical. Its practical work is based on a deep feeling for an inner life in the actor: but in public it denies this life because in a character inner life takes on the dread label 'psychological'. This word 'psychological' is invaluable in coloured argument – like 'naturalistic' it can be used with contempt to close a subject or score a point. Unfortunately, it also leads to a simplification, contrasting the language of action – this language is hard, bright and effective – with the language of psychology – this is Freudian, mushy, shifting, dark, imprecise. Looked at this way, of course psychology must lose. But is the division a true one? Everything is illusion. The exchange of impressions through images is our basic language: at the moment when one man expresses an image at that same instant the other man meets him in belief. The shared association is the language – if the association evokes nothing in the second person, if there is no instant of shared illusion, there is no exchange. Brecht often took the case of a man describing a street accident as a narrative situation – so let us take his example and examine the process of perception that is involved. When someone describes to us a street accident the psychic process is complicated: it can best be seen as a three-dimensional collage with built-in sound, for we experience many unrelated things at once. We see the speaker, we hear his voice, we know where we are and, at one and the same time, we perceive superimposed on top of him the scene he is describing: the vividness and the fullness of this momentary illusion depends on his conviction and skill. It also depends on the speaker's type. If he is a cerebral type, I mean a man whose alertness and vitality is mainly in the head, we will receive more impressions of ideas than of sensations. If he is emotionally free, other currents will also flow so that without any effort or research on his part he will inevitably recreate a fuller image of the street accident that he is remembering, and we will receive it accordingly. Whatever it is, he sends in our direction a complex network of impressions, and as we perceive them, we believe in them, thus losing ourselves in them at least momentarily.

In all communication, illusions materialize and disappear. The Brecht theatre is a rich compound of images appealing for our belief. When Brecht spoke contemptuously of illusion, this was not what he was attacking. He meant the single sustained Picture, the statement that continued after its purpose had been served – like the painted tree. But when Brecht stated there was something in the theatre called illusion, the implication was that there was something else that was not illusion. So illusion became opposed to reality. It would be better if we clearly opposed dead illusion to living illusion, glum statement to lively statement, fossilized shape to moving shadow, the frozen picture to the moving one. What we see most often is a character inside a picture frame surrounded by a three-walled interior set. This is naturally an illusion, but Brecht suggests we watch it in a state of anaesthetized uncritical belief. If, however, an actor stands on a bare stage beside a placard reminding us that this is a theatre, then in basic Brecht we do not fall into illusion, we watch as adults – and judge. This division is neater in theory than in practice.

It is not possible that anyone watching either a naturalistic production of a play of Chekhov or a formalized Greek tragedy should surrender to the belief that he is in Russia or Ancient Thebes. Yet it is sufficient in either case for an actor of power to speak a powerful text for the spectator to be caught up in an illusion, although, of course, he will still know that he is at every instant in a theatre. The aim is not how to avoid illusion – everything is illusion, only some things seem more illusory than other. It is the heavy-handed Illusion that does not begin to convince us. On the other hand, the illusion that is composed by the flash of quick and changing impressions keeps the dart of the imagination at play. This illusion is like the single dot in the moving television picture: it only lasts for the instant its function demands.

It is an easy mistake to consider Chekhov as a naturalistic writer, and in fact many of the sloppiest and thinnest plays of recent years called 'slice of life' fondly think themselves Chekhovian. Chekhov never just made a slice of life – he was a doctor who with infinite gentleness and care took thousands and thousands of fine layers off life. These he cultured, and then arranged them in an exquisitely cunning, completely artificial and meaningful order in which part of the cunning lay in so disguising the artifice that the result looked like the keyhole view it never had been. Any page of *The Three Sisters* gives the impression of life unfolding as though a tape-recorder had been left running. If examined carefully it will be seen to be built of coincidences as great as in Feydeau – the vase of flowers that overturns, the fire-engine that passes at just the right moment; the word, the interruption, the distant music, the sound in the wings, the entrance, the farewell – touch by touch, they create through the language of illusions an overall illusion of a slice of life. This series of impressions is equally a series of alienations: each rupture is a subtle provocation and a call to thought.

I have already quoted performances in Germany after the

war. In a Hamburg garret I once saw a production of *Crime and Punishment*, and that evening became, before its four-hour stretch was over, one of the most striking theatre experiences I have ever had. By sheer necessity, all problems of theatre style vanished: here was the real main stream, the essence of an art that stems from the story-teller looking round his audience and beginning to speak. All the theatres in the town had been destroyed, but here, in this attic, when an actor in a chair touching our knees began quietly to say, 'It was in the year of 18 – that a young student, Roman Rodianovitch Raskolnikov . . .' we were gripped by living theatre.

Gripped. What does that mean? I cannot tell. I only know that these words and a soft serious tone of voice conjured something up, somewhere, for us all. We were listeners, children hearing a bedside story yet at the same time adults, fully aware of all that was going on. A moment later, a few inches away, an attic door creaked open and an actor impersonating Raskolnikov appeared, and already we were deep in the drama. The door at one instant seemed a total evocation of a street lamp; an instant later it became the door of the money-lender's apartment, and still a second later the passage to her inner room. Yet, as these were only fragmentary impressions that only came into being at the instant they were required, and at once vanished again, we never lost sight of being crammed together in a crowded room, following a story. The narrator could add details, he could explain and philosophize, the characters themselves could slip from naturalistic acting into monologue, one actor could, by hunching his back, slip from one characterization to another, and point for point, dot for dot, stroke for stroke, the whole complex world of Dostoevsky's novel was recreated.

How free is the convention of a novel, how effortless the relationship of writer to reader: backgrounds can be evoked and dismissed, the transition from the outer to the inner world is natural and continuous. The success of the Hamburg experiment reminded me again of how grotesquely clumsy, how inadequate and pitiful the theatre becomes, not only when a gang of men and creaking machines are needed to move us only from one place to the next, but even when the transition from the world of action to the world of thought has to be explained by any device – by music, changing lights or clambering on to platforms.

In the cinema, Godard has singlehanded brought about a revolution by showing how relative the reality of a photographed scene can be. Where generations of film-makers had evolved laws of continuity and canons of consistency so as not to break the reality of a continuous action, Godard showed that this reality was yet another false and rhetorical convention. By photographing a scene and at once smashing its apparent truth, he has cracked into dead Illusion and enabled a stream of opposing impressions to stream forth. He is deeply influenced by Brecht.

The Berliner Ensemble's recent production of *Coriolanus* underlines the whole question of where illusion begins and ends. In most respects, this version was a triumph. Many aspects of the play were revealed as though for the first time: much of it can seldom have been so well staged. The company approached the play socially and politically and this meant that the stock mechanical ways of staging Shakespearian crowds were no longer possible. It would have been impossible to get any one of those intelligent actors playing an anonymous citizen merely to make cheers, mutters and jeers on cue like bit players through the ages. The energy that fed the months of work that eventually illuminated all the structure of sub-plot came from the actor's interest in the social themes. The small parts were not boring to the actors – they never became background because they obviously carried issues fascinating to study and provocative to discuss. The people, the tribunes, the battle, the assemblies, were rich in texture: all forms of theatre were pressed into service – the costumes had the feel of everyday life but the stage positions had the formality of tragedy. The speech was sometimes heightened, sometimes colloquial, the battles used ancient Chinese techniques to carry modern meanings. There was not a moment of stock theatricality, nor any noble emotion used for its own sake. Coriolanus was not idealized nor even likeable: he was explosive, violent – not admirable but convincing. Everything served the action which itself was crystal clear.

And then appeared a tiny defect that became for me a deep, interesting flaw. The major confrontation scene between Coriolanus and Volumnia at the gates of Rome was rewritten. I do not for one moment question the principle of rewriting Shakespeare – after all, the texts do not get burned – each person can do what he thinks necessary with a text and still no one suffers. What is interesting is the result. Brecht and his colleagues did not wish to allow the lynch-pin of the entire action to be the relation between Coriolanus and his mother. They felt that this did not make an interesting contemporary point: in its place they wished to illustrate the theme that no leader is indispensable. They invented an additional piece of narrative. Coriolanus demanded the citizens of Rome to give a smoke signal if they were prepared to surrender. At the end of his discussion with his mother he sees a column of smoke rising from the ramparts and is jubilant. His mother points out that the smoke is not a sign of surrender, but the smoke from the forges of the people arming themselves to defend their homes. Coriolanus realizes that Rome can carry on without him and senses the inevitability of his own defeat. He yields.

In theory, this new plot is as interesting and works as well as the old one. But any play of Shakespeare's has an organic sense. On paper it would look as though the episode can reasonably be substituted for another, and certainly in many plays there are scenes and passages that can easily be cut or transposed. But if one has a knife in one hand, one needs a stethoscope in the other. The scene between Coriolanus and his mother is close to the heart of the play: like the storm in Lear or a Hamlet monologue, its emotional content engenders the heat by which strands of cool thought and patterns of dialectical argument are eventually fused. Without the clash of the two protagonists in its most intense form, the story remains castrated. When we leave the theatre we carry a less insistent memory with us. The force of the scene between Coriolanus and his mother depends on just those elements that do not necessarily make apparent sense. Psychological language, also, gets us nowhere, for labels don't count; it is the deeper ring of truth that can command our respect – the dramatic fact of a mystery we can't completely fathom.

The Berliner Ensemble's choice implied that their social attitude would be weakened by accepting the unfathomable nature of the man-within-the-social-scene. Historically it is clear how a theatre loathing the self-indulgent individualism of bourgeois art should have turned to actions instead.

★ ★ ★

In Peking today it seems to make good sense to show giant Wall Street caricature figures plotting war and destruction and getting their just deserts. In relation to countless other factors of today's militant China, this is lively, meaningful popular art. In many South American countries, where the only theatre activity has been poor copies of foreign successes put on by flybynight impresarios, a theatre only begins to find its meaning and its necessity in relation to the revolutionary struggle on the one hand and the glimmers of a popular tradition suggested by workers' songs and village legends on the other. In fact, an expression of today's militant themes through traditional catholic morality-play structures may well be the only possibility in certain regions of finding a lively contact with popular audiences. In England, on the other hand, in a changing society, where nothing is truly defined, least of all in the realm of politics and political ideas; but where there is a constant re-examination in process that varies from the most intensely honest to the most frivolously evasive: when the natural common-sense and the natural idealism, the natural debunking and the natural romanticism, the natural democracy, the natural kindness, the natural sadism and the natural snobbery all make a mishmash of intellectual confusion, it would be no use expecting a committed theatre to follow a party line – even supposing that such a line could be found.

The accumulation of events of the last few years, the assassinations, schisms, downfalls, uprisings and the local wars have had an increasingly demystifying effect. When the theatre comes closest to reflecting a truth in society, it now reflects more the wish for change than the conviction that this change can be brought about in a certain way. Certainly the role of the individual in the society, his duties and his needs, the issues of what belongs to him and what belongs to the state, are in question again. Again, as in Elizabethan times, man is asking why he has a life and against what he can measure it. It is not by chance that the new metaphysical theatre of Grotowski arises in a country drenched in both Communism and Catholicism. Peter Weiss, combining Jewish family, Czech upbringing, German language, Swedish home, Marxist sympathies, emerges just at the moment when his Brechtianism is related to obsessive individualism to a degree unthinkable in Brecht himself. Jean Genet relates colonialism and racialism to homosexuality, and explores the French consciousness through his own degradation. His images are private yet national, and he comes close to discovering myths.

The problem is different for each centre of population. On the whole, though, the stifling effects of a nineteenth-century obsessive interest in middle-class sentiment clouds much twentieth-century work in all languages. The individual and the couple have long been explored in a vacuum or in a social context so insulated as to be the equivalent of a vacuum. The relationship between a man and the evolving society around him is always the one that brings new life depth and truth to his personal theme. In New York and London play after play presents serious leading characters within a softened diluted or unexplored context – so that heroism, self-torture or martyrdom become romantic agonies, in the void.

Whether the emphasis falls on the individual or on the analysis of society has become almost completely a division between marxists and non-marxists. It is the marxist and the marxist alone who approaches a given situation dialectically and scientifically, attempting to explore the social and economic factors that determine the action. There are non-marxist economists and non-marxist sociologists, but any writer who begins to set a historical character fully in his context is almost certain to be working from a marxist point of view. This is because marxism provides the writer with a structure, a tool and an aim – bereft of these three elements the non-marxist turns to Man. This can easily make the writer vague and woolly. But the very best non-political writer may be another sort of expert, who can discriminate very precisely in the treacherous world of individual shades of experience. The epic writer of marxist plays seldom brings to his work this same fine sense of human individuality: perhaps because he is unwilling to regard a man's strength and a man's weakness with equal impartiality. It is perhaps for this reason that strangely the pop tradition in England has such wide appeal: non-political, unaligned, it is none the less tuned in on a fragmented world in which bombs, drugs, God, parents, sex, and private anxieties, are inseparable – and all illuminated by a wish, not a very strong wish, but a wish all the same – for some sort of change or transformation.

There is a challenge to all the theatres in the world who have not yet begun to face the movements of our time, to saturate themselves in Brecht, to study the Ensemble and see all those facets of society that have found no place in their shut-off stages. There is a challenge to revolutionary theatres in countries with a clear-cut revolutionary situation like in Latin America to harness their theatres boldly to unmistakably clear-cut themes. Equally, there is a challenge now to the Berliner Ensemble and its followers to reconsider their attitude to the darkness of individual man. This is our only possibility – to look at the affirmations of Artaud, Meyerhold, Stanislavsky, Grotowski, Brecht, then compare them with the life of the particular place in which we work. What is our purpose, now, in relation to the people we meet every day? Do we need liberation? From what? In what way?

* * *

Shakespeare is a model of a theatre that contains Brecht and

Beckett, but goes beyond both. Our need in the post-Brecht theatre is to find a way forwards, back to Shakespeare. In Shakespeare the introspection and the metaphysics soften nothing. Quite the reverse. It is through the unreconciled opposition of Rough and Holy, through an atonal screech of absolutely unsympathetic keys that we get the disturbing and the unforgettable impressions of his plays. It is because the contradictions are so strong that they burn on us so deeply.

Obviously, we can't whistle up a second Shakespeare. But the more clearly we see in what the power of Shakespearian theatre lies, the more we prepare the way. For example, we have at last become aware that the absence of scenery in the Elizabethan theatre was one of its greatest freedoms. In England at least, all productions for quite some time have been influenced by the discovery that Shakespeare's plays were written to be performed continuously, that their cinematic structure of alternating short scenes, plot intercut with subplot, were all part of a total shape. This shape is only revealed dynamically, that is, in the uninterrupted sequence of these scenes, and without this their effect and power are lessened as much as would be a film that was projected with breaks and musical interludes between each reel. The Elizabethan stage was like the attic I was describing in Hamburg, it was a neutral open platform – just a place with some doors – and so it enabled the dramatist effortlessly to whip the spectator through an unlimited succession of illusions, covering, if he chose, the entire physical world. It has also been pointed out that the nature of the permanent structure of the Elizabethan playhouse, with its flat open arena and its large balcony and its second smaller gallery, was a diagram of the universe as seen by the sixteenth-century audience and playwright – the gods, the court and the people – three levels, separate and yet often intermingling – a stage that was a perfect philosopher's machine.

What has not been appreciated sufficiently is that the freedom of movement of the Elizabethan theatre was not only a matter of scenery. It is too easy to think that so long as a

modern production moves fast from scene to scene, it has
learnt the essential lesson from the old playhouse. The
primary fact is that this theatre not only allowed the playwright to roam the world, it also allowed him free passage
from the world of action to the world of inner impressions. I
think it is here that we find what is most important to us
today. In Shakespeare's time, the voyage of discovery in the
real world, the adventure of the traveller setting out into the
unknown, had an excitement that we cannot hope to recapture
in an age when our planet has no secrets and when the pros-
pect of interplanetary travel seems a pretty considerable bore.
However, Shakespeare was not satisfied with the mysteries
of the unknown continents: through his imagery – pictures
drawn from the world of fabulous discoveries – he penetrates
a psychic existence whose geography and movements remain just as vital for us to understand today.

In an ideal relation with a true actor on a bare stage we
would continually be passing from long shot to close, track-
ing or jumping in and out and the planes often overlap.
Compared with the cinema's mobility, the theatre once
seemed ponderous and creaky, but the closer we move towards the true nakedness of theatre, the closer we approach
a stage that has a lightness and range far beyond film or
television. The power of Shakespeare's plays is that they
present man simultaneously in all his aspects: touch for touch,
we can identify and withdraw. A primitive situation disturbs
us in our subconscious; our intelligence watches, comments,
philosophizes. Brecht and Beckett are both contained in
Shakespeare unreconciled. We identify emotionally, sub-
jectively – and yet at one and the same time we evaluate
politically, objectively in relation to society. Because the profound reaches past the everyday, a heightened language and a
ritualistic use of rhythm brings us to those very aspects of
life which the surface hides: and yet because the poet and the
visionary do not seem like ordinary people, because the
epic state is not one on which we normally dwell, it is
equally possible for Shakespeare with a break in his rhythm,
a twist into prose, a shift into slangy conversation or else a

direct word from the audience to remind us – in plain common-sense – of where we are and to return us to the familiar
rough world of spades as spades. So it is that Shakespeare
succeeded where no one has succeeded before or since in
writing plays that pass through many stages of consciousness.
What enabled him technically to do so, the essence, in fact,
of his style is a roughness of texture and a conscious mingling
of opposites which in other terms could be called an absence
of style. Voltaire could not bring himself to understand it,
and could only label it 'barbaric'.

We could take *Measure for Measure* as a test case. As long
as scholars could not decide whether this play was a comedy
or not, it never got played. In fact, this ambiguity makes it
one of the most revealing of Shakespeare's works – and one
that shows these two elements, Holy and Rough, almost
schematically, side by side. They are opposed and they co-
exist. In *Measure for Measure* we have a base world, a very
real world in which the action is firmly rooted. This is the
disgusting, stinking world of medieval Vienna. The darkness
of this world is absolutely necessary to the meaning of the
play: Isabella's plea for grace has far more meaning in this
Dostoevskian setting than it would in lyrical comedy's
never-never land. When this play is prettily staged, it is
meaningless – it demands an absolutely convincing roughness
and dirt. Also, when so much of the play is religious in
thought, the loud humour of the brothel is important as a
device, because it is alienating and humanizing. From the
fanatical chastity of Isabella and the mystery of the Duke we
are plunged back to Pompey and Barnadine for douches of
normality. To execute Shakespeare's intentions we must
animate all this stretch of the play, not as fantasy, but as the
roughest comedy we can make. We need complete freedom,
rich improvisation, no holding back, no false respect – and at
the same time we must take great care, for all around the
popular scenes are great areas of the play that clumsiness
could destroy. As we enter this holier land, we will find that
Shakespeare gives us a clear signal – the rough is in prose,
the rest in verse. In the prose scenes, very broadly speaking,

the work can be enriched by our own invention – the scenes need added external details to assure them of their fullest life. In the passages in verse we are already on our guard: Shakespeare needs verse because he is trying to say more, to compact together more meaning. We are watchful: behind each visible mark on paper lurks an invisible one that is hard to seize. Technically we now need less abandon, more focus – less breadth, more intensity.

Quite simply we need a different approach, a different style. There is nothing to be ashamed of in changing style – look at a page of a Folio with half-closed eyes and you see a chaos of irregularly spaced symbols. If we iron Shakespeare into any one typography of theatre we lose the real meaning of the play – if we follow his ever-shifting devices, he will lead us through many different keys. If we follow the movement in *Measure for Measure* between the Rough and the Holy we will discover a play about justice, mercy, honesty, forgiveness, virtue, virginity, sex and death: kaleidoscopically one section of the play mirrors the other, it is in accepting the prism as a whole that its meanings emerge. When I once staged the play I asked Isabella, before kneeling for Angelo's life, to pause each night until she felt the audience could take it no longer – and this used to lead to a two-minute stopping of the play. The device became a voodoo pole – a silence in which all the invisible elements of the evening came together, a silence in which the abstract notion of mercy became concrete for that moment to those present.

This Rough/Holy structure also shows clearly in the two parts of *Henry IV* – Falstaff and the prose realism of the inn scenes on the one hand and the poetic levels of so much else – both elements contained within one complex whole.

In *A Winter's Tale* a very subtle construction hinges on the key moment when a statue comes to life. This is often criticized as a clumsy device, an implausible way of winding up the plot, and it is usually justified only in terms of romantic fiction; an awkward convention of the times that Shakespeare was forced to use. In fact, the statue that comes to life is the truth of the play. In *A Winter's Tale* we find a natural division into three sections. Leontes accuses his wife of infidelity. He condemns her to death. The child is put to sea. In the second part the child grows up, and now in a different pastoral key the very same action is repeated. The man falsely accused by Leontes now in turn behaves just as unreasonably. The consequence is the same – the child again takes flight. Her journey takes her back to Leontes' palace and the third part is now in the same place as the first, but twenty years later. Again, Leontes finds himself in similar conditions, in which he could be as violently unreasonable as before. Thus the main action is presented first ferociously; then a second time by charming parody but in a bold major key, for the pastoral of the play is a mirror as well as a straight device. The third movement is in another contrasting key – a key of remorse. When the young lovers enter Leontes' palace the first and second sections overlap: both put into question the action that Leontes now can take. If the dramatist's sense of truth forces him to make Leontes vindictive with the children, then the play cannot move out of its particular world, and its end would have to be bitter and tragic: if he can truthfully allow a new equality to enter Leontes' actions, then the whole time pattern of the play is transformed: the past and the future are no longer the same. The level changes, and even if we call it a miracle, the statue has none the less come to life. When working on *The Winter's Tale* I discovered that the way to understand this scene is not to discuss it but to play it. In performance this action is strangely satisfying – and so it makes us wonder deeply.

Here we have an example of the 'happening' effect – the moment when the illogical breaks through our everyday understanding to make us open our eyes more widely. The whole play has established questions and references: the moment of surprise is a jolt to the kaleidoscope, and what we see in the playhouse we can retain and relate to the play's questions when they recur transposed, diluted and disguised, in life.

If we imagine for a moment *Measure for Measure* and *A Winter's Tale* written by Sartre, it would be reasonable to guess that in the one case Isabella would not kneel for Angelo – so that the play would end with the hollow crackle of the firing squad – and in the other the statue would not come to life, so that Leontes would be faced with the bleak consequences of his actions. Both Shakespeare and Sartre would be fashioning plays according to their sense of truth: one author's inner material contains different intimations from the other's. The mistake would be to take events or episodes from a play and question them in the light of some third outside standard of plausibility – like 'reality' or 'truth'. The sort of play that Shakespeare offers us is never just a series of events: it is far easier to understand if we consider the plays as objects – as many faceted complexes of form and meaning in which the line of narrative is only one amongst many aspects – and cannot profitably be played or studied on its own.

Experimentally, we can approach Lear not as a linear narrative, but as a cluster of relationships. First, we try to rid ourselves of the notion that because the play is called *King Lear* it is primarily the story of one individual. So we pick an arbitrary point in the vast structure – the death of Cordelia, say, and now instead of looking towards the King we turn instead towards the man who is responsible for her death. We focus on this character, Edmund, and now we begin to pick our way to and fro across the play, sifting the evidence, trying to discover who this Edmund is. He is clearly a villain, whatever our standards, for in killing Cordelia he is responsible for the most gratuitous act of cruelty in the play – yet if we look at our first impression of him in the early scenes, we find he is by far the most attractive character we meet. In the opening scenes there is a denial of life in Lear's rusty ironclad power; Gloucester is tetchy, fussy and foolish, a man blind to everything except his inflated image of his own importance; and in dramatic contrast we see the relaxed freedom of his bastard son. Even if in theory we observe that the way he leads Gloucester by the nose is hardly moral, instinctively we cannot but side with his natural anarchy. Not only do we sympathize with Goneril

and Regan for falling in love with him, but we tend to side
with them in finding Edmund so admirably wicked, because
he affirms a life that the sclerosis of the older people seems to
deny. Can we keep this same attitude of admiration towards
Edmund when he has Cordelia killed? If not, why not? What
has changed? Is it Edmund who has changed, through outside
events? Or is it just the context that is different? Is a scale of
value implied? What are Shakespeare's values? What is the
value of a life? We flick through the play again and find an
incident importantly situated, unrelated to the main plot,
often quoted as an example of Shakespeare's slovenly construction. This is the fight between Edmund and Edgar. If
we look closely, we are struck by one fact – it is not the
powerful Edmund, but his younger brother who wins. In the
first scenes of the play, Edmund had no trouble at all in out-
witting Edgar – now five acts later in single combat it is
Edgar who dominates. Accepting this as dramatic truth
rather than romantic convention, we are forced to ask how it
has come about. Can we explain it all quite simply in terms
of moral growth – Edgar has grown up, Edmund has
decayed – or is the whole question of Edgar's undoubted
development from *naïveté* to understanding – and Edmund's
visible change from freedom to entanglement – far more
complex than a cut-and-dried question of the triumph of the
good. Aren't we compelled in fact to relate this to all the
evidence connected with the question of growth and decline,
i.e. youth and age, i.e. strength and weakness. If for a
moment we assume this point of view, then suddenly the
whole play seems concerned with sclerosis opposing the flow
of existence, of cataracts that dissolve, of rigid attitudes that
yield, while at the same time obsessions form and positions
harden. Of course the whole play is also about sight and
blindness, what sight amounts to, what blindness means –
how the two eyes of Lear ignore what the instinct of the Fool
apprehends, how the two eyes of Gloucester miss what his
blindness knows. But the object has many facets; many
themes criss-cross its prismatic form. Let us stay with the
strands of age and youth, and in pursuit of them move on to

the very last lines of the play. When we read or hear them first our reaction is, 'How obvious. What a trite end', for Edgar says:

> 'We that are young
> Shall never see so much, nor live so long'.

The more we look at them the more troubling they become, because their apparent precision vanishes, making way for a strange ambiguity hidden in the naïve jangle. The last line is, at its face value, plain nonsense. Are we to understand that the young will never grow up, or are we to understand that the world will never again know old men? Both of these seems a pretty feeble winding up by Shakespeare of a consciously written masterpiece. However, if we look back through Edgar's own line of action, we see that although Edgar's experience in the storm parallels Lear's, it certainly has not wrought in him the intense inner change that has taken place in Lear. Yet Edgar acquired the strength for two killings – first Oswald, then his brother. What has this done to him – how deeply has he experienced this loss of innocence? Is he still wide-eyed? Is he saying in his closing words that youth and age are limited by their own definitions – that the only way to see as much as Lear is to go through Lear's mill, and then *ipso facto* one is young no longer. Lear lives longer than Gloucester – in time and in depth – and as a result he undoubtedly 'sees' more than Gloucester before he dies. Does Edgar wish to say that it is experience of this order and intensity that really means 'living long'. If so, the 'being young' is a state with its own blindness – like that of the early Edgar, and its own freedom like that of the early Edmund. Age in turn has its blindness and decay. However, true sight comes from an acuteness of living that can transform the old. Indeed, it is clearly shown to us in the unfolding of the play that Lear suffers most and 'gets farthest'. Undoubtedly, his brief moment of captivity with Cordelia is as a moment of bliss, peace and reconciliation, and Christian commentators often write as though this were the end of the story – a clear tale of the ascent from the inferno through purgation to paradise. Unfortunately for this neat view the play continues, pitilessly, away from reconciliation.

> 'We that are young
> Shall never see so much, nor live so long.'

The power of Edgar's disturbing statement – a statement that rings like a half-open question – is that it carries no moral overtones at all. He does not suggest for one moment that youth or age, seeing or not seeing, are in any way superior, inferior, more desirable or less desirable one than the other. In fact we are compelled to face a play which refuses all moralizing – a play which we begin to see not as a narrative any longer, but as a vast, complex, coherent poem designed to study the power and the emptiness of nothing – the positive and negative aspects latent in the zero. So what does Shakespeare mean? What is he trying to teach us? Does he mean that suffering has a necessary place in life and is worth cultivating for the knowledge and inner development it brings? Or does he mean us to understand that the age of titantic suffering is now over and our role is that of the eternally young? Wisely, Shakespeare refuses to answer. But he has given us his play, and its whole field of experience is both question and answer. In this light, the play is directly related to the most burning themes of our time, the old and the new in relation to our society, our arts, our notions of progress, our way of living our lives. If the actors are interested, this is what they will bring out. If we are interested, that is what we will find. Fancy dress, then, will be left far behind. The meaning will be for the moment of performance.

Of all the plays, none is so baffling and elusive as *The Tempest*. Again, we discover that the only way to find a rewarding meaning in it is to take it as a whole. As a straight-forward plot it is uninteresting; as a pretext for costumes, stage effects and music it is hardly worth reviving; as a pot-pourri of knockabout and pretty writing it can at best please a few matinée-goers – but usually it only serves to put generations of school children off theatre for life. But when we see how nothing in the play is what it seems, how it takes place on an

island and not on an island, during a day and not during a
day, with a tempest that sets off a series of events that are
still within a tempest even then the storm is done, that the
charming pastoral for children naturally encompasses rape,
murder, conspiracy and violence; when we begin to unearth
the themes that Shakespeare so carefully buried, we see that
it is his complete final statement, and that it deals with the
whole condition of man. In a similar way, Shakespeare's first
play *Titus Andronicus* begins to yield its secrets the moment
one ceases to regard it as a string of gratuitous strokes of
melodrama and begins to look for its completeness. Everything in Titus is linked to a dark flowing current out of which
surge the horrors, rhythmically and logically related – if one
searches in this way one can find the expression of a powerful
and eventually beautiful barbaric ritual. But in Titus this un-
earthing is comparatively simple – today we can always find
our way to the violent sub-conscious. *The Tempest* is another
matter. From first play to last, Shakespeare moved through
many limbos: maybe the conditions cannot be found today
for the play's nature to be revealed fully. Until, however, a
way of presenting it can be found, we can at least be wary of
confusing unsuccessful attempts at wrestling with the text
with the thing itself. Even if unplayable today, it remains an
example of how a metaphysical play can find a natural idiom
that is holy, comic and rough.

* * *

So it is that in the second half of the twentieth century in
England where I am writing these words, we are faced with
the infuriating fact that Shakespeare is still our model. In this
respect, our work on Shakespeare production is always to
make the plays 'modern' because it is only when the audience
comes into direct contact with the plays' themes that time and
conventions vanish. Equally, when we approach the modern
theatre, in whatever form, whether the play with a few
characters, the happening, or the play with hordes of characters and scenes, the problem is always the same – where are
the equivalents to the Elizabethan strengths, in the sense of

range and stretch. What form, in modern terms, could that rich theatre take? Grotowski, like a monk who finds a universe in a grain of sand, calls his holy theatre a theatre of poverty. The Elizabethan theatre that encompassed all of life including the dirt and the wretchedness of poverty is a rough theatre of great richness. The two are not nearly as far apart as they might seem.

I have talked a lot about inner and outer worlds, but like all oppositions it is a relative one, a convenience of notation. I have talked about beauty, magic, love: knocking these words with one hand, seeming to reach towards them with the other. And yet the paradox is a simple one. All that we see connected with these words seems deadly: what they imply corresponds to what we need. If we do not understand catharsis, that is because it has become identified with an emotional steam bath. If we do not understand tragedy, it is because it has become confused with Acting The King. We may want magic, but we confuse it with hocus-pocus, and we have hopelessly mixed up love with sex, beauty with aestheticism. But it is only by searching for a new discrimination that we will extend the horizons of the real. Only then could the theatre be useful, for we need a beauty which could convince us: we need desperately to experience magic in so direct a way that our very notion of what is substantial could be changed.

It is not as though the period of necessary debunking were now over. On the contrary, all through the world in order to save the theatre almost everything of the theatre still has to be swept away. The process has hardly begun, and perhaps can never end. The theatre needs its perpetual revolution. Yet wanton destruction is criminal; it produces violent reaction and still greater confusion. If we demolish a pseudo-holy theatre, we must endeavour not to bamboozle ourselves into thinking that the need for the sacred is old-fashioned and that cosmonauts have proved once and for all that angels do not exist. Also, if we get dissatisfied with the hollowness of so much of the theatre of revolutionaries and propagandists, we must not for this reason assume that the need to talk of people, of power, of money and of the structure of society is a passing fashion.

But if our language must correspond with our age, then we must also accept that today roughness is livelier and holiness deadlier than at other times. Once, the theatre could begin as magic: magic at the sacred festival, or magic as the footlights came up. Today, it is the other way round. The theatre is hardly wanted and its workers are hardly trusted. So we cannot assume that the audience will assemble devoutly and attentively. It is up to us to capture its attention and compel its belief.

To do so we must prove that there will be no trickery, nothing hidden. We must open our empty hands and show that really there is nothing up our sleeves. Only then can we begin.

4

The Immediate Theatre

THERE is no doubt that a theatre can be a very special place. It is like a magnifying glass, and also like a reducing lens. It is a small world, so it can easily be a petty one. It is different from everyday life so it can easily be divorced from life. On the other hand, while we live less and less in villages or neighbourhoods, and more and more in open-ended global communities, the theatre community stays the same: the cast of a play is still the size that it has always been. The theatre narrows life down. It narrows it down in many ways. It is always hard for anyone to have one single aim in life – in the theatre, however, the goal is clear. From the first rehearsal, the aim is always visible, not too far away, and it involves everyone. We can see many model social patterns at work: the pressure of a first night, with its unmistakable demands, produce that working-together, that dedication, that energy and that consideration of each other's needs that government despair of ever evoking outside wars.

Furthermore, in society in general the role of art is nebulous. Most people could live perfectly well without any art at all – and even if they regretted its absence it would not hamper their functioning in any way. But in the theatre there is no such separation: at every instant the practical question is an artistic one: the most incoherent, uncouth player is as much involved in matters of pitch and pace, intonation and rhythm, position, distance, colour and shape as the most sophisticated. In rehearsal, the height of the chair, the texture of the costume, the brightness of the light, the quality of emotion, matter all the time: the aesthetics are practical. One would be wrong to say that this is because the theatre is an art. The stage is a reflection of life, but this life cannot be re-lived for a moment without a working system based on observing certain values and making value-judgements. A chair is moved up or down stage, because it's 'better so'. Two columns are wrong – but adding a third makes them 'right' – the words 'better', 'worse', 'not so good', 'bad' are day after day, but these words which rule decisions carry no moral sense whatsoever.

Anyone interested in processes in the natural world would be very rewarded by a study of theatre conditions. His discoveries would be far more applicable to general society than the study of bees or ants. Under the magnifying glass he would see a group of people living all the time according to precise, shared, but un-named standards. He would see that in any community a theatre has either no particular function – or a unique one. The uniqueness of the function is that it offers something that cannot be found in the street, at home, in the pub, with friends, or on a psychiatrist's couch; in a church or at the movies. There is only one interesting difference between the cinema and the theatre. The cinema flashes on to a screen images from the past. As this is what the mind does to itself all through life, the cinema seems intimately real. Of course, it is nothing of the sort – it is a satisfying and enjoyable extension of the unreality of everyday perception. The theatre, on the other hand, always asserts itself in the present. This is what can make it more real than the normal stream of consciousness. This also is what can make it so disturbing.

No tribute to the latent power of the theatre is as telling as that paid to it by censorship. In most régimes, even when the written word is free, the image free, it is still the stage that is liberated last. Instinctively, governments know that the living event could create a dangerous electricity – even if we see this happen all too seldom. But this ancient fear is a recognition of an ancient potential. The theatre is the arena where a living confrontation can take place. The focus of a large group of people creates a unique intensity – owing to this forces that operate at all times and rule each person's daily life can be isolated and perceived more clearly.

Now, I must become unashamedly personal. In the three preceding chapters I have dealt with different forms of theatre, in general, as they occur all over the world, and naturally as they occur to me. If this final section, which inevitably is a sort of conclusion, takes the form of a theatre I appear to recommend, this is because I can only speak of the theatre I know. I must narrow my sights and talk about theatre as I understand it, autobiographically. I will endeavour to speak of actions and conclusions from within my field of work: this is what constitutes my experience and my point of view. In turn, the reader must observe that it is inseparable from all the things on my passport – nationality, date of birth, place of birth, physical characteristics, colour of eyes, signature. Also, it is inseparable from today's date. This is a picture of the author at the moment of writing: searching within a decaying and evolving theatre. As I continue to work, each experience will make these conclusions inconclusive again. It is impossible to assess the function of a book – but I hope this one may perhaps be of use somewhere, to someone else wrestling with his own problems in relation to another time and place. But if anyone were to try to use it as a handbook, then I can definitely warn him – there are no formulas: there are no methods. I can describe an exercise or a technique, but anyone who attempts to reproduce them from my description is certain to be disappointed. I would undertake to teach anyone all that I know about theatre rules and technique in a few hours. The rest is practice – and that cannot be done alone. We can just attempt to follow this to a limited degree if we examine the preparation of a play towards performance.

* * *

In performance, the relationship is actor/subject/audience. In rehearsal it is actor/subject/director. The earliest relationship is director/subject/designer. Scenery and costumes can sometimes evolve in rehearsal at the same time as the rest of the performance, but often practical considerations of building and dress-making force the designer to have his work cut and dried before the first rehearsal. I have often done my own designs. This can be a distinct advantage, but for a very special reason. When the director is working this way, his theoretical understanding of the play and its extension in terms of shapes and colours both evolve at the same tempo. A scene may escape the director for several weeks, one shape in the set may seem incomplete – then as he works on the set he may suddenly find the place of the scene that eludes him; as he works on the structure of the difficult scene he may suddenly glimpse its meaning in terms of stage action or a succession of colours. In work with a designer, a sympathy of tempo is what matters most. I have worked with joy with many marvellous designers – but have at times been caught in strange traps, as when the designer reaches a compelling solution too fast – so that I found myself having to accept or refuse shapes before I had sensed what shapes seemed to be immanent in the text. When I accepted the wrong shape, because I could find no logical reason for opposing the designer's conviction, I locked myself into a trap out of which the production could never evolve, and produced very bad work as a result. I have often found that the set is the geometry of the eventual play, so that a wrong set makes many scenes impossible to play, and even destroys many possibilities for the actors. The best designer evolves step by step with the director, going back, changing, scrapping, as a conception of the whole gradually takes form. A director who does his own designs naturally never believes that the completion of the designs can be an end in itself. He knows that he is just at the beginning of a long cycle of growth, because his own work lies before him. Many designers, however, tend to feel that with the delivery of the sets and costume sketches a major portion of their own creative work in genuinely complete. This particularly applies to good painters working in the theatre. For them, a completed design is complete. Art lovers can never understand why all stage designing isn't done by 'great' painters and sculptors. What is necessary, however, is an incomplete design; a design that has clarity without rigidity;

one that could be called 'open' as against 'shut'. This is the
essence of theatrical thinking: a true theatre designer will
think of his designs as being all the time in motion, in action,
in relation to what the actor brings to a scene as it unfolds. In
other words, unlike the easel painter, in two dimensions, or
the sculptor in three, the designer thinks in terms of the
fourth dimension, the passage of time – not the stage picture,
but the stage moving picture. A film editor shapes his
material after the event: the stage designer is often like the
editor of an Alice-Through-the-Looking-Glass film, cutting
dynamic material in shapes, before this material has yet come
into being. The later he makes his decisions, the better.

It is very easy – and it happens quite often – to spoil an
actor's performance with the wrong costume. The actor who
is asked his views about a costume design before rehearsals
start is in a similar position to the director who is asked for a
decision before he is ready. He has not yet had a physical
experience of his role – so his views are theoretical. If the
designer sketches with panache – and if the costume is beautiful in its own right – the actor will often accept it with enthusiasm, only to discover weeks later that it is out of tune
with all that he is trying to express. Fundamental to the
work of designing is the problem – what should an actor
wear? A costume doesn't just come out of the designer's
head: it springs from a background. Take the situation of a
white European actor playing a Japanese. Even if every con-
trivance is used, his costume will never have the allure of a
Samurai in a Japanese film. In the authentic setting, the
details are right and related to one another: in the copy based
on a study of documents, there is almost inevitably a steady
series of compromises; the material is only more or less the
same, the detail of the cut adapted and approximate, eventually the actor himself is unable to inhabit the costume with
the instinctive rightness of the men close to the source.

If we cannot present a Japanese or an African satisfactorily
by processes of imitation, the same holds good for what we
call 'period'. An actor whose work seems real in rehearsal
clothes easily loses this integrity when dressed in a toga

copied from a vase in the British Museum. Yet wearing everyday clothes is seldom the answer, they are usually inadequate as a uniform for performance. The Noh theatre, for instance, has preserved ritual performing clothes that are of great beauty, and so has the Church. In baroque periods, a contemporary 'finery' existed –and so could be the base of clothing for play or opera. The romantic ball was still recently a valid source for remarkable designers like Oliver Messel or Christian Bérard. In the U.S.S.R. after the Revolution, the white tie and tails, dropped from social life, still supplied the formal basis for clothing musicians aptly and elegantly in a manner that separated the performance from the rehearsal.

For us every time we start a new production we are compelled to reopen this question as though for the first time. What can the actors wear? Is there a period implied in the action? What is a 'period'? What is its reality? Are the aspects given to us by documents real? Or is some flight of fancy and inspiration more real? What is the dramatic purpose? What needs clothing? What needs stating? What, physically, does the actor require? What does the eye of the spectator demand? Should this demand of the spectator be met harmoniously or opposed, dramatically? What can colour and texture heighten? What might they blur?

Casting creates a new set of problems. If rehearsals are short, type casting is inevitable – but everyone deplores it, naturally. In re-action, every actor wants to play everything. In fact, he can't: each actor is eventually blocked by his own true limits, which outline his real type. All one can say is that most attempts to decide in advance what an actor can *not* do are usually abortive. The interest in actors is their capacity for producing unsuspected traits in rehearsal: the disappointment in an actor is when he is true to form. To try to cast 'knowingly' is usually a vanity: it is better to have the time and conditions in which it is possible to take risks. One may often be wrong – but in exchange these will be quite unexpected revelations and developments. No actor stands completely still in his career. It is easy to imagine that he has got stuck at a certain level, when in fact a considerable unseen change is under way inside him. The actor who seems very good at an audition may be very talented, but on the whole this is unlikely – he is more probably just efficient and his effectiveness is only skin-deep. The actor who seems very bad at an audition is most likely the worst actor present, but this is not necessarily the case, and it is just possible he is the best. There is no scientific way round this: if the system dictates the employing of actors one doesn't know, one is forced to work largely by guesswork.

At the beginning of rehearsals the actors are the opposite of the ideally relaxed creatures they would like to be. They bring with them a heavy baggage of tensions. So varied are these tensions that we can find some very unexpected phenomena. For instance, a young actor playing with a group of inexperienced friends may reveal a talent and a technique that put professionals to shame. Yet take the very same actor who has, as it were, proved his worth and surround him with the older actors he most respects, and often he becomes not only awkward and stiff, but even his talent goes. Put him then amongst actors he despises and he will come into his own again. For talent is not static, it ebbs and flows according to many circumstances. Not all actors of the same age are at the same stage of their professional work. Some have a blend of enthusiasm and knowledge that is supported by a confidence based on previous small successes and is not undermined by fear of imminent total failure. They start rehearsals from a different position from the perhaps equally young actor who has made a slightly greater name and who is already beginning to wonder how much farther he can go – has he really got anywhere yet, what is his status, is he recognized, what does the future hold? The actor who believes he may one day play Hamlet has endless energy: the one who sees that the outside world is not convinced he will ever play a lead is already tying himself into painful knots of introspection with a consequent need for self-assertion.

In the group that gathers for a first rehearsal, whether a scratch cast or a permanent company, an infinite number of personal questions and worries hang unspoken in the air. Of course, these are all enhanced by the presence of the director: if he were in a God-sent state of total relaxation he could greatly help, but more of the time he too is tense and involved with the problems of his production and here too the need publicly to deliver the goods is fuel to his own vanity and his self-absorption. In fact, a director can never afford to begin with his first production. I remember hearing that a budding hypnotist never confesses to a subject that he is hypnotizing for the first time. He has 'done it successfully many times'. I began with my second production, because when at seventeen I faced my first group of sharp and critical amateurs, I was forced to invent a non-existent just completed triumph to give them and myself the confidence we both required.

The first rehearsal is always to a degree the blind leading the blind. On the first day a director may sometimes make a formal speech explaining the basic ideas behind the coming work. Or else he may show models or costume sketches, or books or photographs, or he may make jokes, or else get the actors to read the play. Having drinks or playing a game together or marching round the theatre or building a wall all work in the same way: no one is in a state to absorb what is said – the purpose of anything you do on the first day is to get you through to the second one. The second day is already different – a process is now at work, and after twenty-four hours every single factor and relationship has subtly changed. Everything you do in rehearsal affects this process: playing games together is a process that has certain results, like a greater feeling of confidence, friendliness and informality. One can play games at auditions just to bring about an easier atmosphere. The goal is never in the game alone – in the short time available for rehearsing a play, social ease is not enough. A harrowing collective experience – like the improvisations on madness we had to do for the *Marat/Sade* brings about another result; the actors having shared difficulties are open to one another and to the play in a different way.

A director learns that the growth of rehearsals is a developing process; he sees that there is a right time for everything, and his art is the art of recognizing these moments. He learns that he has no power to transmit certain ideas in the early days. He will come to recognize the look on the face of an apparently relaxed but innerly anxious actor who cannot follow what he is being told. He will then discover that all he needs is to wait, not push too hard. In the third week all will have changed, and a word or a nod will make instant communication. And the director will see that he too does not stay still. However much home-work he does, he cannot fully understand a play by himself. Whatever ideas he brings on the first day must evolve continually, thanks to the process he is going through with the actors, so that in the third week he will find that he is understanding everything differently. The actors' sensibilities turn searchlights on to his own – and he will either know more, or at least see, more vividly that he has so far discovered nothing valid.

In fact, the director who comes to the first rehearsal with his script prepared with the moves and business, etc., noted down, is a real deadly theatre man.

When Sir Barry Jackson asked me to direct *Love's Labour's Lost* at Stratford in 1945, it was my first big production and I had already done enough work in smaller theatres to know that actors, and above all stage managers, had the greatest contempt for anyone who, as they always put it, 'did not know what he wanted'. So the night before the first rehearsal I sat agonized in front of a model of the set, aware that further hesitation would soon be fatal, fingering folded pieces of cardboard – forty pieces representing the forty actors to whom the following morning I would have to give orders, definite and clear. Again and again, I staged the very first entry of the Court, recognizing that this was when all would be lost or won, numbering the figures, drawing charts, manœuvring the scraps of cardboard to and fro, on and off the set, trying them in big batches, then in small, from the side, from the back, over grass mounds, down steps, knocking them all over with my sleeve, cursing and starting again. As

I did so, I noted the moves, and with no one to notice my indecision, crossed them out, then made fresh notes. The next morning I arrived at rehearsal, a fat prompt book under my arm, and the stage management brought me a table, reacting to my volume, I observed, with respect.

I divided the cast into groups, gave them numbers and sent them to their starting places, then, reading out my orders in a loud confident way I let loose the first stage of the mass entrance. As the actors began to move I knew it was no good. These were not remotely like my cardboard figures, these large human beings thrusting themselves forward, some too fast with lively steps I had not foreseen, bringing them suddenly on top of me – not stopping, but wanting to go on, staring me in the face: or else lingering, pausing, even turning back with elegant affectations that took me by surprise – we had only done the first stage of the movement, letter A on my chart, but already no one was rightly placed and movement B could not follow – my heart sank and, despite all my preparation, I felt quite lost. Was I to start again, drilling these actors so that they conformed to my notes? One inner voice prompted me to do so, but another pointed out that my pattern was much less interesting than this new pattern that was unfolding in front of me – rich in energy, full of personal variations, shaped by individual enthusiasms and lazinesses, promising such different rhythms, opening so many unexpected possibilities. It was a moment of panic. I think, looking back, that my whole future work hung in the balance. I stopped, and walked away from my book, in amongst the actors, and I have never looked at a written plan since. I recognized once and for all the presumption and the folly of thinking that an inanimate model can stand for a man.

Of course, all work involves thinking: this means comparing, brooding, making mistakes, going back, hesitating, starting again. The painter naturally does this, so does the writer, but in secret. The theatre director has to expose his uncertainties to his cast, but in reward he has a medium which evolves as it responds: a sculptor says that the choice of material continually amends his creation: the living material of actors is talking, feeling and exploring all the time – rehearsing is a visible thinking-aloud.

Let me quote a strange paradox. There is only one person as effective as a very good director – and that is a rotten one. It sometimes happens that a director is so bad, so completely without direction, so incapable of imposing his will, that his lack of ability becomes a positive virtue. It drives the actors to despair. Gradually his incompetence makes a gulf that yawns in front of the cast, and as the first night approaches insecurity gives way to terror, which becomes a force. It has happened that in the last moments a company found a strength and a unity as though by magic – and they gave a first-night performance for which the director got high praise. Equally, when a director is fired, the new man taking over often has an easy job: I once entirely re-staged someone else's production in the course of one night – and got unfair credit for the result. Despair had so prepared the ground that a touch from one finger was all that was required.

However, when the director is plausible enough, stern enough, articulate enough to get the actors' partial trust, then the result can misfire easiest of all. Even if the actor ends by disagreeing with some of what he is told, he still passes some of the load on to the director feeling that 'he may be right', or at least that the director is vaguely 'responsible' and will somehow 'save the day'. This spares the actor the final personal responsibility and prevents the conditions for the spontaneous combustion of a company coming into being. It is the modest director, the honourable unassuming one, often the nicest man, who should be trusted least.

What I am saying can very easily be misunderstood – and directors who do not wish to be despots are sometimes tempted to the fatal course of doing nothing, cultivating non-intervention in the belief that this is the only way of respecting the actor. This is a wretched fallacy – without leadership a group cannot reach a coherent result within a given time. A director is not free of responsibility – he is totally responsible – but he is not free of the process either, he is part of it.

Every now and then an actor turns up who proclaims that directors are unnecessary: actors could do it by themselves. This may be true. But what actors? For actors to develop something alone, they would need to be creatures so highly developed that they would hardly need rehearsal either; they would read the script and in a wink the invisible substance of the play would appear fully articulated amongst them. This is unreal: a director is there to help a group evolve towards this ideal situation. The director is there to attack and yield, provoke and withdraw until the indefinable stuff begins to flow. The anti-director wants the director out of the way from the first rehearsal: any director disappears, a little later, on the first night. Sooner or later the actor must appear and the ensemble take command. The director must sense where the actor wants to go and what it is he avoids, what blocks he raises to his own intentions. No director injects a performance. At best a director enables an actor to reveal his own performance, that he might otherwise have clouded for himself.

Acting begins with a tiny inner movement so slight that it is almost completely invisible. We see this when we compare film and stage acting: a good stage actor can act in films, not necessarily vice versa. What happens? I make a proposition to an actor's imagination such as, 'She is leaving you.' At this moment deep in him a subtle movement occurs. Not only in actors – the movement occurs in anyone, but in most non-actors the movement is too slight to manifest itself in any way: the actor is a more sensitive instrument and in him the tremor is detected – in the cinema the great magnifier, the lens, describes this to the film that notes it down, so for the cinema the first flicker is all. In early theatre rehearsals, the impulse may get no further than a flicker – even if the actor wishes to amplify it all sorts of extraneous psychic psychological tensions can intervene – then the current is short-circuited, earthed. For this flicker to pass into the whole organism, a total relaxation must be there, either god-given or brought about by work. This, in short, is what rehearsals are all about. In this way acting is mediumistic – the idea

suddenly envelops the whole in an act of possession – in Grotowski's terminology the actors are 'penetrated' – penetrated
by themselves. In very young actors, the obstacles are sometimes very elastic, penetration can happen with surprising
ease and they can give subtle and complex incarnations that are
the despair of those who have evolved their skill over years.
Yet later, with success and experience, the same young actors
build up their barriers to themselves. Children can often act
with extraordinary natural technique. People from real life
are marvellous on screen. But with adult professionals there
has to be a two-way process, and the stirring from within
has to be aided by the stimulus from outside. Sometimes
study and thought can help an actor to eliminate the preconceptions that blind him to deeper meanings, but sometimes it
is the reverse. To reach an understanding of a difficult role,
an actor must go to the limits of his personality and intelligence – but sometimes great actors go farther still if they
rehearse the words and at the same time listen acutely to the
echoes that arise in them.

   John Gielgud is a magician – his form of theatre is one
that is known to reach above the ordinary, the common, the
banal. His tongue, his vocal chords, his feeling for rhythm
compose an instrument that he has consciously developed all
through his career in a running analogy with his life. His
natural inner aristocracy, his outer social and personal beliefs,
have given him a hierarchy of values, an intense discrimination between base and precious, and a conviction that the
sifting, the weeding, the selecting, the dividing, the refining
and the transmuting are activities that never end. His art
has always been more vocal than physical: at some early
stage in his career he decided that for himself the body was a
less supple instrument than the head. He thus jettisoned part
of an actor's possible equipment but made true alchemy with
the rest. It is not just speech, not melodies, but the continual movement between the word-forming mechanism and
his understanding that has made his art so rare, so touching
and especially so aware. With Gielgud, we are conscious
both of what is expressed and of the skill of the creator:

that a craft can be so deft adds to our admiration. The experience of working with him has been amongst my most special and my greatest joys.

Paul Scofield talks to his audience in another way. While in Gielgud the instrument stands half-way between the music and the hearer, and so demands a player, trained and skilled – in Scofield, instrument and player are one – an instrument of flesh and blood that opens itself to the unknown. Scofield, when I first knew him as a very young actor, had a strange characteristic: verse hampered him, but he would make unforgettable verse out of lines of prose. It was as though the act of speaking a word sent through him vibrations that echoed back meanings far more complex than his rational thinking could find: he would pronounce a word like 'night' and then he would be compelled to pause: listening with all his being to the amazing impulses stirring in some mysterious inner chamber, he would experience the wonder of discovery at the moment when it happened. Those breaks, those sallies in depth, give his acting its absolutely personal structure of rhythms, its own instinctive meanings: to rehearse a part, he lets his whole nature – a milliard of super-sensitive scanners – pass to and fro across the words. In performance the same process makes everything that he has apparently fixed come back again each night the same and absolutely different.

I use two well-known names as illustrations, but the phenomenon is there all the time in rehearsal, and continually reopens the problem of innocence and experience, of spontaneity and knowledge. There are also things young actors and unknown actors can do that have passed beyond the reach of fine actors with experience and skill.

There have been times in theatre history when the actor's work has been based on certain accepted gestures and expressions: there have been frozen systems of attitudes which we reject today. It is perhaps less obvious that the opposite pole, the Method Actor's freedom in choosing anything whatsoever from the gestures of everyday life is equally restricted, for in basing his gestures on his observation or on his own spontaneity the actor is not drawing on any deep creativity. He is reaching inside himself for an alphabet that is also fossilized, for the language of signs from life that he knows is the language not of invention but of his conditioning. His observations of behaviour are often observations of projections of himself. What he thinks to be spontaneous is filtered and monitored many times over. Were Pavlov's dog improvising, he would still salivate when the bell rang, but he would feel sure it was all his own doing: 'I'm dribbling,' he would say, proud of his daring

Those who work in improvisation have the chance to see with frightening clarity how rapidly the boundaries of so-called freedom are reached. Our exercises in public with the Theatre of Cruelty quickly led the actors to the point where they were nightly ringing variations on their own clichés – like Marcel Marceau's character who breaks out of one prison to find himself within another. We experimented for instance with an actor opening a door and finding something unexpected. He had to react to the unexpected sometimes in gesture, sometimes in sound, sometimes with paint. He was encouraged to express the first gesture, cry or splash that came to him. At first, all this showed was the actor's stock of similies. The open mouth of surprise, the step back in horror: where did these so-called spontaneities come from? Clearly the true and instantaneous inner reaction was checked and like lightning the memory substituted some imitation of a form once seen. Dabbing the paint was even more revealing: the hair's-breadth of terror before the blankness, and then the reassuring ready-made idea coming to the rescue. This Deadly Theatre lurks inside us all.

The aim of improvisation in training actors in rehearsal, and the aim of exercises, is always the same: it is to get away from Deadly Theatre. It is not just a matter of splashing about in self-indulgent euphoria as outsiders often suspect; for it aims at bringing the actor again and again to his own barriers, to the points where in place of new-found truth he normally substitutes a lie. An actor playing a big scene falsely appears false to the audience because, instant for instant, in his progression from one attitude of the character to another, he is substituting false details for real ones: tiny transitional phoney emotions through imitation attitudes. But this cannot be grappled with while rehearsing big scenes – too much is going on, it is far too complicated. The purpose of an exercise is to reduce and return: to narrow the area down and down until the birth of a lie is revealed and caught. If the actor can find and see this moment he can perhaps open himself to a deeper, more creative impulse.

Similarly, when two actors play together. What we know most is external ensemble playing: much of the teamwork of which the English theatre is so proud is based on politeness, courtesy, reasonableness, give-and-take, your turn, after you, and so on – a facsimile which works whenever the actors are in the same range of style – i.e. older actors play beautifully together, and so do very young ones; but when they are mixed up, for all their care and mutual respect, the result is often a mess. For a production I did of Genet's *The Balcony* in Paris it was necessary to mix actors of very different backgrounds – classically trained, film trained, ballet trained and simple amateur. Here, long evenings of very obscene brothel improvisations served only one purpose – they enabled this hybrid group of people to come together and begin to find a way of responding directly to one another.

Some exercises open the actors to one another in a quite different way: for example, several actors may play completely different scenes side by side, but never speaking at the same moment, so that each has to pay close attention to the whole, in order to know just what moments depended on him. Or else developing a collective sense of responsibility for the quality of an improvisation, and switching to new situations as soon as the shared invention flags. Many exercises set out first to free the actor, so he may be allowed to discover by himself what only exists in himself: next, to force him to accept blindly external directions, so that by cocking a sensitive enough ear he could hear in himself movements he would never have detected any other way. For instance a valuable exercise is dividing a Shakespeare soliloquy into three voices, like a canon, and then having the three actors recite at breakneck speed over and over again. At first, the technical difficulty absorbs all the actors' attention, then gradually as they master the difficulties they are asked to bring out the meaning of the words, without varying the inflexible form. Because of the speed and the mechanical rhythm this seems impossible: the actor is prevented from using any of his normal expressive equipment. Then suddenly he bursts a barrier and experiences how much freedom there can be within the tightest discipline.

Another variant is to take the two lines 'To be or not to be, That is the question' and give them to ten actors, one word each. The actors stand in a closed circle and endeavour to play the words one after the other, trying to produce a living phrase. This is so difficult that it instantly reveals even to the most unconvinced actor how closed and insensitive he is to his neighbour. When after long work the sentence suddenly flows, a thrilling freedom is experienced by everyone. They see in a flash the possibility of group playing, and the obstacles to it. This exercise can be developed by substituting other verbs for 'be', with the same effect of affirmation and denial – and eventually it is possible to put sounds or gestures in place of one or all of the words and still maintain a living dramatic flow between the ten participants.

The purpose of such exercises is to lead actors to the point where if one actor does something unexpected but true, the others can take this up and respond on the same level. This is ensemble playing: in acting terms it means ensemble creation, an awesome thought. It is no use thinking that exercises belong to school and only apply to a certain period of the actor's development. An actor like any artist, is like a garden and it is no help to pull out the weeds just once, for all time. The weeds always grow, this is quite natural, and they must be cleaned away, which is natural and necessary too.

Actors must study by varying means: an actor has mainly an act of elimination to make. Stanislavsky's title 'Building a Character' is misleading – a character isn't a static thing and it can't be built like a wall. Rehearsals don't lead progressively to a first night. This is something very hard for some actors to understand – especially those who pride themselves most on their skill. For mediocre actors the process of character building is as follows: they have an acute moment of artistic anguish, at the very start – 'What will happen this time?' – 'I know I've played many successful parts before but, this time, will inspiration come?' This actor comes in terror to the first rehearsal, but gradually his standard practices fill the vacuum of his fear: as he 'discovers' a way of doing each section, he battens it down, relieved that once again he has been spared the final catastrophe. So on the first night although he is nervous, his nerves are those of the marksman who knows he can hit the target but is afraid he won't get a bull's-eye again when his friends are watching.

The really creative actor reaches a different and far worse terror on the first night. All through rehearsals he has been exploring aspects of a character which he senses always to be partial, to be less than the truth – so he is compelled, by the honesty of his search, endlessly to shed and start again. A creative actor will be most ready to discard the hardened shells of his work at the last rehearsal because here, with the first night approaching, a brilliant searchlight is cast on his creation, and he sees its pitiful inadequacy. The creative actor also longs to cling on to all he's found, he too wants at all costs to avoid the trauma of appearing in front of an audience, naked and unprepared – still this is exactly what he must do. He must destroy and abandon his results even if what he picks up seems almost the same. This is easier for French actors than for English ones, because temperamentally they are more open to the idea that nothing is any good. And this is the only way that a part, instead of being built, can be born. The role that has been *built* is the same every night – except that it slowly erodes. For the part that is born to be the same it must always be reborn, which makes it always different. Of course, particularly in a long run, the effort of daily re-creation becomes unbearable and unthinkable, and this is where the experienced creative artist is compelled to fall back on a second level called technique to carry him through.

I did a play with that perfectionist Alfred Lunt. In the first act, he had a scene sitting on a bench. In rehearsal, he suggested, as a piece of natural business, taking off his shoe and rubbing his foot. Then he added shaking the shoe to empty it before putting it back on again. One day when we were on tour in Boston, I walked past his dressing-room. The door was ajar. He was preparing for the performance, but I could see that he was looking out for me. He beckoned excitedly. I went into the dressing-room, he closed the door, asked me to sit down. 'There's something I want to try tonight,' he said. 'But only if you agree. I went for a walk on Boston Common this afternoon and found these.' He held out his palm. It contained two tiny pebbles. 'That scene were I shake out my shoe,' he continued, 'its always worried me that nothing falls out. So I thought I'd try putting the pebbles in. Then when I shake it, you'd see them drop – and you'd hear the sound. What do you think?' I said it was an excellent idea and his face lit up. He looked delightedly at the two little stones, back at me, then suddenly his expression changed. He studied the stones again for a long anxious moment. 'You don't think it would be better with one?'

The hardest task of all for an actor is to be sincere yet detached – it is drummed into an actor that sincerity is all he needs. With its moral overtones, the word causes great confusion. In a way, the most powerful feature of the Brecht actors is the degree of their *insincerity*. It is only through detachment that an actor will see his own clichés. There is a dangerous trap in the word sincerity. First of all, a young actor discovers that his job is so exacting that it demands of him certain skills. For instance, he has to be heard: his body has to obey his wishes: he must be a master of his timing, not the slave of haphazard rhythms. So he searches for technique: and soon he acquires a know-how. Easily, know-now can become a pride and an end in itself. It becomes dexterity without any other aim than the display of expertise – in other words, the art becomes insincere. The young actor observes the insincerity of the old-timer and is disgusted. He searches for sincerity. Sincerity is a loaded word: like cleanliness it carries childhood associations of goodness, truth-telling and decency. It seems a good ideal, a better aim than acquiring more and more technique, and as sincerity is a feeling, one can always tell when one's being sincere. So there is a path one can follow; one can find one's way to sincerity by emotional 'giving', by being dedicated, by honesty, by taking a no-holds-barred approach and by, as the French say, 'plunging into the bath'. Unfortunately, the result can easily be the worst kind of acting. With any of the other arts, however deep one plunges into the act of creating, it is always possible to step away and look at the result. As the painter steps back from his canvas other faculties can spring into play and warn him at once of his excesses. The trained pianist's head is physically less involved than his fingers and so however 'carried away' he is by the music, his ear carries its own degree of detachment and objective control. Acting is in many ways unique in its difficulties because the artist has to use the treacherous, changeable and mysterious material of himself as his medium. He is called upon to be completely involved while distanced – detached without detachment. He must be sincere, he must be insincere: he must practise how to be insincere with sincerity and how to lie truthfully. This is almost impossible, but it is essential and easily ignored. All too often, actors – and it is not their fault, but that of the deadly schools with which the world is littered – build their work on fag-ends of doctrine. The great system of Stanislavsky, which for the first time approached the whole art of acting from the point of view of science and knowledge, has done as much harm as good to many young actors, who misread it in detail and only take away a good hatred of the shoddy. After Stanislavsky, Artaud's equally significant writings, half-read and a tenth digested, have led to a naïve belief that emotional commitment and unhesitating self-exposure are all that really count. This is now fed further by ill-digested, misunderstood bits of Grotowski. There is now a new form of sincere acting which consists of living everything through the body. It is a kind of naturalism. In naturalism, the actor tries sincerely to imitate the emotions and actions of the everyday world and to live his role. In this other naturalism the actor gives himself over just as completely to living his unrealistic behaviour, through and through. This is where he fools himself. Just because the type of theatre he's connected with seems poles removed from old-fashioned naturalism, he believes that he, too, is far from this despised style. In fact, he approaches the landscape of his own emotions with the same belief that every detail must be photographically reproduced. So he is always at full flood. The result is often soft, flabby, excessive and unconvincing.

There are groups of actors, particularly in the United States, nourished on Genet and Artaud, who despise all forms of naturalism. They would be very indignant if they were called naturalistic actors, but this is precisely what limits their art. To commit every fibre of one's being into an action may seen a form of total involvement – but the true artistic demand may be even more stringent than total involvement –and need fewer manifestations or quite different ones. To understand this, we must see that along with the emotion there is always a role for a special intelligence, that is not there at the start, but which has to be developed as a selecting instrument. There is a need for detachment, in particular, there is a need for certain forms: all of which is hard to define, but impossible to ignore. For instance, actors can pretend to fight with total abandon and genuine violence. Every actor is prepared for death scenes – and he throws himself into them with such abandon that he does not realize he knows nothing at all about death.

In France an actor comes to an audition, asks to be shown the most violent scene in the play and without a qualm plunges into it to demonstrate his paces. The French actor playing a classical part pumps himself up in the wings then plunges into the scene: he judges the success or failure of the evening by the degree he can surrender to his emotions, whether his inner charge is at its maximum pitch and from this comes a belief in the Muse, in inspiration and so on. The weakness of his work is that this way he tends to play generalizations. By this I mean that in an angry scene he gets on to his note of anger – or rather he plugs into his anger-point and this force drives him through the scene. This may give him a certain force and even at times a certain hypnotic power over the audience, and this power is falsely considered to be 'lyrical' and 'transcendental'. In fact, such an actor in his passion becomes its slave and is unable to drop out of the passion if a subtle change of text demands something new. In a speech that contains both natural and lyrical elements he declaims everything as though all the words were equally pregnant. It is this clumsiness that makes actors appear stupid and grand acting seem unreal.

Jean Genet wishes the theatre to come out of the banal, and he wrote a series of letters to Roger Blin when Blin was directing *The Screens*, urging him to push the actors towards 'lyricism'. This sounds well enough in theory but what is lyricism? What is 'out of the ordinary' acting? Does it dictate a special voice, a high-blown manner? Old classical actors seem to sing their lines, is this the relic of some valid old tradition? At what point is a search for form an acceptance of artificiality? This is one of the greatest problems we face today, and so long as we retain any sneaking belief that grotesque masks, heightened make-ups, hieratic costumes, declamation, balletic movement are somehow 'ritualistic' in their own right and consequently lyrical and profound – we will never get out of a traditional art-theatre rut.

At least one can see that everything is a language for something and nothing is a language for everything. Every action happens in its own right and every action is an analogy of something else. I crumple a piece of paper: this gesture is complete in itself: I can stand on a stage and what I do need be no more than what appears at the moment of the happening. It can also be a metaphor. Anyone who saw Patrick Magee slowly tearing strips of newspaper precisely as in life and yet utterly ritualistically in Pinter's *The Birthday Party* will know what this means. A metaphor is a sign and is an illustration – so it is a fragment of language. Every tone of speech, every rhythmic pattern is a fragment of language and corresponds to a different experience. Often, nothing is so deadly

as a well-schooled actor speaking verse: there are of course
academic laws of prosody and they can help to clarify certain
things for an actor at a certain stage of his development, but
he must eventually discover that the rhythms of each character are as distinctive as thumbprints: then he must learn that
every note in the musical scale corresponds – what to?
That also he must find.

Music is a language related to the invisible by which a
nothingness suddenly is there in a form that cannot be seen
but can certainly be perceived. Declamation is not music, yet
it corresponds to something different from ordinary speech:
Sprechgesang also; Carl Orff has set Greek tragedy on to a
heightened level of rhythmic speech supported and punctuated
by percussion and the result is not only striking, it is essentially different from tragedy spoken and tragedy sung: it
speaks of a different thing. We can separate neither the structure nor the sound of Lear's 'Never never never never never'
from its complex of meanings, and we cannot isolate Lear's
'Monster Ingratitude' without seeing how the shortness of
the line of verse brings a tremendous thick emphasis on to
the syllables. There is a moving beyond words in 'Monster
Ingratitude'. The texture of language is reaching towards
the experiences that Beethoven imitated in patterns of
sound – yet it is not music, it cannot be abstracted from its
sense. Verse is deceptive.

An exercise we once developed involved taking a scene of
Shakespeare's, such as Romeo's farewell to Juliet, and trying
(artificially of course) to disentangle the different inter-
twining styles of writing. The scene reads:

Juliet: Wilt thou be gone? It is not yet near day.
It was the nightingale, and not the lark,
That pierced the fearful hollow of thine ear.
Nightly she sing on yond pomegranate tree.
Believe me, love, it was the nightingale.

Romeo: It was the lark, the herald of the morn;
No nightingale. Look, love, what envious streaks

Do lace the severing clouds in yonder East.
Night's candles are burnt out, and jocund day
Stands tiptoe on the misty mountains tops.
I must be gone and live, or stay and die.

Juliet: Yond light is not daylight; I know it, I.
It is some meteor that the sun exhales
To be to thee this night a torchbearer
And light thee on thy way to Mantua.
Therefore stay yet. Thou needest not to be gone.

Romeo: Let me be ta'en, let me be put to death.
I am content, so thou wilt have it so.
I'll say yon grey is not the morning's eye;
'Tis but the pale reflex of Cynthia's brow.
Nor that is not the lark whose notes do beat
The vaulty heaven so high above our heads.
I have more care to stay than will to go.
Come, death, and welcome! Juliet wills it so.
How is't, my soul? Let's talk. It is not day.

The actors then were asked to select only those words that
they could play in a realistic situation, the words that they
could use unselfconsciously in a film. This produced:

Juliet: Wilt thou be gone? It is not yet near day.
It was the nightingale [*pause*] not the lark [*pause*]

Romeo: It was the lark [*pause*] no nightingale. Look,
love [*pause*] I must be gone and live, or stay
and die.

Juliet: Yond light is no daylight; [*pause*] therefore
stay yet. Thou needest not to be gone.

Romeo: Let me be ta'en, let me be put to death. I
am content, so thou wilt have it so. [*pause*]
Come, death and welcome! Juliet wills it so.
How is't, my soul? Let's talk. It is not
day.

Then the actors played this as a genuine scene from a modern play full of living pauses – speaking the selected words out loud, but repeating the missing words silently to themselves to find the uneven lengths of the silences. The fragment of scene that emerged would have made good cinema, for the moments of dialogue linked by a rhythm of silences of unequal duration in a film would be sustained by close shots and other silent, related images.

Once this crude separation had been made, it was then possible to do the reverse: to play the erased passages with full recognition that they had nothing whatsoever to do with normal speech. Then it was possible to explore them in many different ways – turning them into sounds or movements – until the actor saw more and more vividly how a single line of speech can have certain pegs of natural speech round which twist unspoken thoughts and feelings rendered apparent by words of another order. This change of style from the apparently colloquial to the evidently stylized is so subtle that it cannot be observed by any crude attitudes. If the actor approaches a speech looking for its form, he must beware not to decide too easily what is musical, what is rhythmic. It is not enough for an actor playing Lear in the storm, to take a running jump at the speeches, thinking of them as splendid slabs of storm music. Nor is it any use speaking them quietly for their meaning on the grounds that they are actually taking place inside his head. A passage of verse can be understood more like a formula carrying many characteristics – a code in which each letter has a different function. In the storm speeches, the explosive consonants are there to suggest by imitation the explosive pattern of thunder, wind and rain. But the consonants are not everything: within these crackling letters writhes a meaning, a meaning that's ever on the change, a meaning that's carried by meaning's bearer, images. Thus, 'you cataracts and hurricanes spout' is one thing 'All germens spill at once That make Ingrateful man', is quite another. With writing as compact as this, the last degree of skill is needed: any loud actor can roar both lines with the same noise, but the artist

must not only present to us with absolute clarity the Hiero-
nymous Bosch – Max Ernst-like image in the second line of
the heavens spilling their spermatozoa, he must present this
within the context of Lear's own rage. He will observe
again that the verse gives great weight to 'That make Ingrateful man', this will reach him as a very precise stage
direction from Shakespeare himself, and he will sense and
grope for a rhythmic structure that enables him to give to
these four words the strength and weight of a longer line
and in so doing hurl on to the longshot of man in storm a
tremendous close-up of his absolute belief in human ingratitude. Unlike a close-up in the cinema, this sort of close-up,
close-up with an idea, frees us from an exclusive pre-occupa-
tion with the man himself. Our complex faculties engage more
fully and in our minds we place Ingrateful man over Lear and
over the world, his world, our world, at one and the same
time.

Yet this is the point where we most need to keep touch with
common-sense, where the right artifice turns stilted or bom-
bastic, 'Have a whisky' – the content of this phrase clearly is
better rendered by a conversational tone of voice than by
song. 'Have a whisky', this phrase we would agree has only
one dimension, one weight, one function. Yet in *Madame
Butterfly* these words are sung and indirectly Puccini's one
phrase has brought the whole form of opera into ridicule.
'Dinner, ho!' in Lear's scene with his knights is similar to
'Have a whisky'. Lears often declaim this phrase, bringing
the play into artificialities, yet when Lear says the words, he
is not acting in a poetic tragedy, he is simply a man calling
for his dinner. 'Ingrateful man' and 'Dinner, ho!' are both
lines by Shakespeare in a verse tragedy, but in fact they belong to quite different worlds of acting.

In rehearsal, form and content have to be examined sometimes together, sometimes separately. Sometimes an exploration of the form can suddenly open us up to the meaning that
dictated the form – sometimes a close study of content gives
us a fresh sound of rhythm. The director must look for where
the actor is messing up his own right urges – and here he

must help the actor to see and overcome his own obstacles. All this is a dialogue and a dance between director and player. A dance is an accurate metaphor, a waltz between director, player and text. Progression is circular, and deciding who's the leader depends on where you stand. The director will find that all the time new means are needed: he will discover that any rehearsal technique has its use, that no technique is all-embracing. He will follow the natural principle of rotation of crops: he will see that explanation, logic, improvisation, inspiration, are methods that rapidly run dry and he will move from one to the other. He will know that thought, emotion, and body can't be separated – but he will see that a pretended separation must often take place. Some actors do not respond to explanation, while others do. This differs in each situation, and one day it is unexpectedly the non-intel-lectual actor who responds to a word from the director, while the intellectual understands all from a gesture.

In early rehearsals, improvisation, exchange of associa-tions and memories, reading of written material, reading of period documents, looking at films and at paintings can all serve to stimulate the material relevant to the theme of a play inside each individual. None of these methods means much in itself – each is a stimulus. In the *Marat/Sade*, as kinetic images of insanity rose up and possessed the actor and as he yielded to them in improvisation, the others observed and criticized. So a true form was gradually detached from the standardized clichés that are part of an actor's equipment for mad scenes. Then as he produced an imitation of madness that convinced his fellows by its seeming reality, he had to come up against a new problem. He may have used an image from observation, from life, but the play is about madness as it was in 1808 – before drugs, before treatment, when a dif-ferent social attitude to the insane made them behave differently, and so on. For this, the actor had no outside model – he looked at faces in Goya not as models to imitate but as prods to encourage his confidence in following the stronger and more worrying of his inner impulses. He had to allow himself to serve these voices completely; and in parting from outside models, he was taking greater risks. He had to cultivate an act of possession. As he did so, he faced a new difficulty, his responsibility to the play. All the shaking, juddering and roaring, all the sincerity in the world can still get the play nowhere. He has lines to speak – if he invents a character incapable of speaking them he will be doing his job badly. So the actor has to face two opposite requirements. The temptation is to compromise – to tone down the impulses of the character to suit the stage needs. But his real task lies in the opposite direction. Make the character vivid – and functional. How? It is just there that the need for intelligence arises.

There is a place for discussion, for research, for the study of history and documents as there is a place for roaring and howling and rolling on the floor. Also, there is a place for relaxation, informality, chumminess, but also there is a time for silence and discipline and intense concentration. Before his first rehearsal with our actors, Grotowski asked for the floor to be swept and for all clothes and personal belongings to be taken out of the room. Then he sat behind a desk, speaking to the actors from a distance, allowing neither smoking nor conversation. This tense climate made certain experiences possible. If one reads Stanislavsky's books, one sees that some of the things said are purely to evoke a seriousness from an actor at a time when the majority of theatres were slipshod. Yet at times, nothing is more liberating than informality and the chucking away of all holy, high-minded ways. Sometimes all the attention must be given to one actor; at other times the collective process demands a halt to the individual's work. Not every facet can be explored. To discuss every possible way with everyone can be just too slow and so it can be destructive to the whole. Here the director has to have a sense of time: it is for him to feel the rhythm of the process and observe its divisions. There is a time for discussing the broad lines of a play, there is a time for forgetting them, for discovering what can only be found through joy, extravagance, irresponsibility. There is a time when no one must worry himself about the results of his efforts. I hate letting people watch rehearsals because I believe that the work is privileged, thus private: there must be no concern about whether one is being foolish or making mistakes. Also a rehearsal may be incomprehensible – often excesses can be left or encouraged even to the amazement and dismay of the company until the moment is ripe to call a halt. But even in rehearsal there is a time when one needs outside people watching, when what always seem to be hostile faces can create a good new tension and the tension a new focus: the work must all the time set new demands. There is another point the director must sense. He must sense the time when a group of actors intoxicated by their own talent and the excitement of the work loses sight of the play. Suddenly one morning the work must change: the result must become all important. Jokes and embroideries are then ruthlessly pared away and all the attention put on to the function of the evening, on the narrating, the presenting, the technique, the audibility, the communicating to the audience. So it is foolish for a director to take a doctrinaire view; either talking technical language about pace, volume, etc. – or avoiding one because it is inartistic. It is woefully easy for a director to get stuck in a method. There comes a moment when talk about speed, precision, diction is all that counts. 'Speed up', 'get on with it', 'it's boring', 'vary the pace', 'for Christ's sake' is then the patter, yet a week before such old-timer talk could have stultified all creativity.

The closer the actor approaches the task of performing, the more requirements he is asked to separate, understand and fulfil simultaneously. He must bring into being an unconscious state of which he is completely in charge. The result is a whole, indivisible – but emotion is continually illuminated by intuitive intelligence so that the spectator, though wooed, assaulted, alienated and forced to reassess, ends by experiencing something equally indivisible. Catharsis can never have been simply an emotional purge: it must have been an appeal to the whole man.

Now the moment of performance, when it comes, is reached through two passageways – the foyer and the stage

door. Are these, in symbolic terms, links or are they to be
seen as symbols of separation? If the stage is related to life, if
the auditorium is related to life, then the openings must be
free and open passageways must allow an easy transition
from outside life to meeting place. But if the theatre is essentially artificial, then the stagedoor reminds the actor that he is
now entering a special place that demands costume, make up,
disguise, change of identity – and the audience also dresses
up, so as to come out of the everyday world along a red carpet
into a place of privilege. Both of these are true and both must
be carefully compared, because they carry quite different
possibilities with them and relate to quite different social
circumstances. The only thing that all forms of theatre have
in common is the need for an audience. This is more than a
truism: in the theatre the audience completes the steps of
creation. In the other arts, it is possible for the artist to use
as his principle the idea that he works for himself. However
great his sense of social responsibility, he will say that his
best guide is his own instinct – and if he is satisfied when
standing alone with his completed work, the chances are that
other people will be satisfied too. In the theatre this is modified by the fact that the last lonely look at the completed
object is not possible – until an audience is present the object
is not complete. No author, no director, even in a megalomaniac dream, would want a private performance, just for
himself. No megalomaniac actor would want to play for
himself, for his mirror. So for the author or the director to
work for his own taste and his own judgement, he must work
approximately for himself in rehearsal and only truly for
himself when he is hemmed in by a dense bank of audience.
I think any director will agree that his own view of his own
work changes completely when he is sitting surrounded by
people.

   Seeing a first public performance of a play one has directed
is a strange experience. Only a day before, one sat at a run-
through and was completely convinced that a certain actor
was playing well, that a certain scene was interesting, a
movement graceful, a passage full of clear and necessary

meaning. Now surrounded by audience part of oneself is responding like this audience, so it is oneself who is saying 'I'm bored', 'he's said that already', 'if she moves once more in that affected way I'll go mad' and even 'I don't understand what they're trying to say'. Apart from the over-sensibility brought about by nerves, what actually is happening to make such a startling change in the director's view of his own work? I think that it is above all a question of the order in which the events now occur. Let me explain this by a single example. In the first scene of a play a girl meets her lover. She has rehearsed with great tenderness and truth and invests a simple greeting with an intimacy that touches everyone – out of context. In front of an audience, it suddenly becomes clear the the preceding lines and actions have in no way prepared for this: in fact, the audience may be busy trying to pick up quite different trails relating to other characters and themes – then suddenly it is faced with a young actress murmuring half inaudibly to a young man. In a later scene, the sequence of events could have led to a hush in which this murmuring would be exactly right – here it seems half-hearted, the intention unclear and even incomprehensible.

The director tries to preserve a vision of the whole, but he rehearses in fragments and even when he sees a run-through it is unavoidably with foreknowledge of all the play's intentions. When an audience is present, compelling him to react as an audience, this foreknowledge is filtered away and for the first time he find himself receiving the impressions given by the play in their proper time-sequence, one after another. Not surprisingly he finds that everything appears different.

For this reason any experimenter is concerned with all aspects of his relationships with an audience. He tries by placing the audience in different positions to bring about new possibilities. An apron stage, an arena, a fully lit house, a cramped barn or room – already these condition different events. But the difference may be superficial: a more profound difference can arise when the actor can play on a

changing inner relationship with the spectator. If the actor
can catch the spectator's interest, thus lower his defences and
then coax the spectator to an unexpected position or an awareness of a clash of opposing beliefs, of absolute contradictions,
then the audience becomes more active. This activity does not
demand manifestations – the audience that answers back may
seem active, but this may be quite superficial – true activity can
be invisible, but also indivisible.

The one thing that distinguishes the theatre from all the
other arts is that it has no permanence. Yet it is very easy
to apply – almost from force of critical habit – permanent
standards and general rules to this ephemeral phenomenon.
One night in an English provincial town, Stoke-on-Trent, I
saw a production of *Pygmalion*, staged in a theatre-in-the-
round. The combination of lively actors, lively building,
lively audience, brought out the most sparkling elements of
the play. It 'went' marvellously. The audience participated
fully. The performance was triumphantly complete. The cast
were all too young for their parts: they had unconvincing
grey lines painted on their hair and very obvious make-ups.
If by magic they had been transported that very instant to
the West End of London and found themselves surrounded
by a London audience in a conventional London building
they would have seemed unconvincing and the audience
would have been unconvinced. However, this does not mean
that the London standard is better or higher than the provincial one. It is more likely to be the reverse, because
it is unlikely that anywhere in London that evening the
theatrical temperature was nearly so high as in Stoke. But
the comparison can never been made. The hypothetical 'if'
can never be put to the test, when it's not just the actors or
the script, but the whole of the performance that one is
assessing.

At the Theatre of Cruelty part of our study was the
audience, and our very first public performance was an
interesting experience. The audience that came to see an 'experimental' evening arrived with the usual mixture of condescension, playfulness and faint disapproval that the notion

of the *avant-garde* arouses. We presented to them a number
of fragments. Our own purpose was uniquely selfish – we
wanted to see some of our experiments in performance conditions. We did not give the audience a programme, list of
authors, of names, of items, nor any commentary or explanation of our own intentions.

The programme began with Artaud's three-minute play,
The Spurt of Blood, made more Artaud than Artaud because
his dialogue was entirely replaced by screams. Part of the
audience was immediately fascinated, part giggled. We meant
it seriously, but next we played a little interlude that we
ourselves considered a joke. Now the audience was lost: the
laughers did not know whether to laugh any more, the
serious-minded who had disapproved of their neighbours'
laughter no longer knew what attitude to take. As the performance continued, the tension grew: when Glenda Jackson,
because a situation demanded it, took off all her clothes a new
tension came into the evening because the unexpected now
might have no bounds. We could observe how an audience
is in no way prepared to make its own instant judgements
second for second. At the second performance the tension was
no longer the same. There were no reviews, and I do not
believe that many people on the second night had been
primed by friends who had come the night before. Yet the
audience was less tense. Rather I think that other factors
were at work – they *knew* we had already performed once
before and the fact that there was *nothing* in the papers in
itself telegraphed a reassurance. The ultimate horrors could
not have taken place – if one of the audience had been injured
– if we had set fire to the building, then it would have been on
the front page. No news was good news. Then as the run
wore on, word of mouth got around that there were improvisations, some dull bits, a chunk of Genet, a shake-up of
Shakespeare, some loud sounds and so the audience arrived,
selected, because of course some now preferred to stay at
home, and gradually only the enthusiasts or the determined
scoffers filtered through. Whenever one has a real critical
flop, for the remainder of the run there is always a small

audience of great enthusiasm – and on the last night of a 'failure' there are always cheers. Everything helps to condition an audience. Those who go to a theatre despite bad notices go with a certain wish, a certain expectation; they are prepared, if only for the worst. Almost always we take our places in a theatre with an elaborate set of references conditioning us before the performance begins: when the play ends, we are automatized into getting up and leaving straight away. When at the end of 'U S' we offered the audience the possibility of silence, of sitting still for a while if it wanted – it was interesting to see how this possibility offended some and gratified others. In fact, there is no reason why one should be hustled from a theatre the moment the action is done, and after 'U S' many people sat still for ten minutes or more, then began spontaneously to speak to one another. This seems to me to be more natural and more healthy an end to a shared experience then rushing away – unless the rushing away is also an act of choice, not of social habit.

Today, the question of the audience seems to be the most important and difficult one to face. We find that the usual theatre audience is usually not a very lively one, certainly not a particularly loyal one, so we set off in search of a 'new' audience. This is surely understandable – and yet at the same time rather artificial. On the whole it is true that the younger an audience, the more swift and free its reactions. It is true that on the whole what alienates young people from the theatre is what is bad in theatre anyway, so in changing our forms to woo the young we would seem to be killing two birds with one stone. An observation that can easily be checked at football matches and dog races is that a popular audience is far more vivid in its responses than a middle-class one. So again it would seem to make sense to woo the popular audience through a popular idiom.

But this logic easily breaks down. The popular audience exists and yet it is something of a will-o'-the-wisp. When Brecht was alive, it was the intellectuals of West Berlin who flocked to his theatre in the East. Joan Littlewood's support came from the West End, and she never found a working-class audience from her own district large enough to carry her through difficult times. The Royal Shakespeare Theatre sends groups out to factories and youth clubs – following Continental patterns – to sell the notion of theatre to those sections of society who have perhaps never set foot in a theatre and are perhaps convinced that theatre is not for them. These commandos aim at evoking interest, breaking down barriers, making friends. This is splendid, stimulating work. But behind it lurks an issue perhaps too dangerous to touch – what truly are they selling? We are implying to a working man that theatre is part of Culture – that is to say, part of the big new hamper of goods now available to everyone. Behind all attempts to reach new audiences there is a secret patronage – 'you too can come to the party' – and like all patronage, it conceals a lie. The lie is the implication that the gift is worth receiving. Do we truly believe in its worth? When people, whose age or class has kept them away from theatres, are lured into them, is it enough to give them 'the best?' The Soviet Theatre attempts to give 'the best'. National Theatres offer 'the best'. At the Metropolitan Opera in New York in a brand-new building the best of Europe's singers under the baton of the best Mozart conductor, and organized by the best producer, play a *Magic Flute*. Apart from the music and the acting, on a recent occasion the cup of culture was really filled to the brim because a splendid series of paintings by Chagall were also displayed scene by scene at the same time. According to the addictive view of culture, it would be impossible to go further – the young man privileged to take his girl to the *Magic Flute* reaches the pinnacle of what his community can offer in terms of the civilized life. The ticket is 'hot' – but what is the evening worth? In a sense, all forms of audience wooing flirt dangerously with this same proposition – come and share in the good life which is good, because it has to be good, because it contains the best.

This can never really change so long as culture or any art is simply an appendage on living, separable from it and, once separated, obviously unnecessary. Such art then is only fought for by the artist to whom, temperamentally, it is necessary, for it is his life. In the theatre we always return to the same point: it is not enough for writers and actors to experience this compulsive necessity, audiences must share it, too. So in this sense it is not just a question of wooing an audience. It is an even harder matter of creating works that evoke in audiences an undeniable hunger and thirst.

A true image of necessary theatre-going I know is a psychodrama session in an asylum. Let us examine for a moment the conditions that prevail there. There is a small community, which leads a regular, monotonous life. On certain days, for some of the inmates, there is an event, something unusual, something to look forward to, a session of drama. When they come into the room where the session is to take place, they know that whatever is going to happen is different from what happens in the wards, the garden, the television room. They all sit in a circle. At the start, they are often suspicious, hostile, withdrawn. The doctor in charge takes the initiative and asks the patients to propose themes. Suggestions are made, they are discussed and slowly there emerge points that interest more than one patient, points that literally become points of contact. Conversation develops painfully around these subjects and the doctor will at once pass to dramatizing them. In the circle, soon, everyone will have his role – but this does not mean that everyone is performing. Some will naturally step forward as protagonists, while others will prefer to sit and watch, either identifying with the protagonist, or following his actions, detached and critical.

A conflict will develop: this is true drama because the people on their feet will be speaking about true issues shared by all present in the only manner that can make these issues really come to life. They may laugh. They may cry. They may not react at all. But behind all that goes on, amongst the so-called insane, lurks a very simple, very sane basis. They all share a wish to be helped to emerge from their anguish, even if they don't know what this help may be, or what form it could take. At this point, let me make it clear that I have no views at all on the value of psychodrama as a treatment. Perhaps it has no lasting medical result at all. But in the immediate event there is an unmistakable result. Two hours after any session begins all the relations between the people present are slightly modified, because of the experience in which they have been plunged together. As a result, something is more animated, something flows more freely, some embryonic contacts are being made between previously sealed-off souls. When they leave the room, they are not quite the same as when they entered. If what has happened has been shatteringly uncomfortable, they are invigorated to the same degree as if there have been great outbursts of laughter. Neither pessimism nor optimism apply: simply, some participants are temporarily, slightly, more alive. If, as they go out of the door, this all evaporates, it does not matter either. Having had this taste, they will wish to come back for more. The drama session will seem an oasis in their lives.

This is how I understand a necessary theatre; one in which there is only a practical difference between actor and audience, not a fundamental one.

As I write, I do not know whether it is only on a tiny scale, in tiny communities, that drama can be renewed. Or whether it is possible on a large scale, in a big playhouse in a capital city. Can we find, in terms of present need, what Glyndebourne and Bayreuth achieved in quite other circumstances, with quite different ideals? That is to say, can we produce homogeneous work that shapes its audience before it has even passed through its doors? Glyndebourne and Bayreuth were in tune with their society and the classes to whom they catered. Today, it is hard to see how a vital theatre and a necessary one can be other than out of tune with society – not seeking to celebrate the accepted values, but to challenge them. Yet the artist is not there to indict, nor to lecture, nor to harangue, and least of all to teach. He is a part of 'them'. He challenges the audience truly when he is the spike in the side of an audience that is determined to challenge itself. He celebrates with an audience most truly when he is the mouthpiece of an audience that has a ground of joy.

Were new phenomena to come into being in front of an audience, and were the audience open to them, a powerful confrontation would occur. Were this to occur, the scattered nature of social thinking would gather round certain bass notes; certain deep aims would be refelt, renewed, reasserted. In this way the divisions between positive and negative experience, between optimism and pessimism, would become meaningless.

At a time when all sands are shifting, the search is automatically a search for form. The destruction of old forms, the experimenting with new ones: new words, new relationships, new places, new buildings: they all belong to the same process, and any individual production is just a separate shot at an unseen target. It is foolish today to expect any single production, group, style or line of work to reveal what we're looking for. The theatre can only advance crabwise in a world whose moving forward is as often sideways as backwards. This is why for a very long time there cannot possibly be a world style for a world theatre – as there was in the theatres and opera houses of the nineteenth century.

But all is not movement, all is not destruction, all is not restlessness, all is not fashion. There are pillars of affirmation. Those are the moments of achievement which do occur, suddenly, anywhere: the performances, the occasions when collectively a total experience, a total theatre of play and spectator makes nonsense of any divisions like Deadly, Rough and Holy. At these rare moments, the theatre of joy, of catharsis, of celebration, the theatre of exploration, the theatre of shared meaning, the living theatre are one. But once gone, the moment is gone and it cannot be recaptured slavishly by imitation – the deadly creeps back, the search begins again.

Every cue to action has a call back to inertia within it. Take that holiest of experiences – music. Music is the one thing that makes life tolerable for a great number of people. So many hours of music a week remind people that life could be worth living – but these instants of solace blunt the edge of their dissatisfaction and so make them more ready to accept an otherwise intolerable way of life. Take the shocking atrocity stories, or the photo of the napalmed child, these shocks are the roughest of experiences – but they open the spectators' eyes to the need for an action which in the event they somehow sap. It is as though the fact of experiencing a need vividly quickens this need and quenches it in the same breath. What then can be done?

I know of one acid test in the theatre. It is literally an acid test. When a performance is over, what remains? Fun can be forgotten, but powerful emotion also disappears and good arguments lose their thread. When emotion and argument are harnessed to a wish from the audience to see more clearly into itself – then something in the mind burns. The event scorches on to the memory an outline, a taste, a trace, a smell – a picture. It is the play's central image that remains, its silhouette, and if the elements are rightly blended this silhouette will be its meaning, this shape will be the essence of what it has to say. When years later I think of a striking theatrical experience I find a kernel engraved on my memory: two tramps under a tree, an old woman dragging a cart, a sergeant dancing, three people on a sofa in hell – or occasio1ally a trace deeper than any imagery. I haven't a hope of remembering the meanings precisely, but from the kernel I can reconstruct a set of meanings. Then a purpose will have been served. A few hours could amend my thinking for life. This is almost but not quite impossible to achieve.

The actor himself is hardly ever scarred by his efforts. Any actor in his dressing-room after playing a tremendous, horrifying role is relaxed and glowing. It is as though the passage of strong feelings through someone engaged in strong physical activity is very healthy. I believe it is good for a man to be an orchestral conductor, good for him to be a tragedian: as a race, they seem consistently to reach a ripe old age. But I also think that there is a price. The material you use to create these imaginary people who you can pick up and discard like a glove is your own flesh and blood. The actor is giving of himself all the time. It is his possible growth, his possible understanding that he is exploiting, using this material to weave these personalities which drop away when the play is done. Our question here is whether anything at all can prevent the same thing happening to the audience. Can the audience retain a mark of its catharsis – or is a glow of well-being the very best it can ever reach?

Even here there are many contradictions. The act of theatre is a release. Both laughter and intense feelings clear some debris from the system – in this way they are the opposite of tracemakers, for like all purgations they make all clean and new. Yet are the experiences that free and the experiences that remain so completely different? Isn't it a verbal naïvety to believe that one is opposed to the other? Isn't it truer to say that in a renewal all things are possible again?

There are many pink old men and women. There are those who have astonishing vigour, but who are great babies: un-lined in face and nature: jolly, but not grown-up. There are also other old people, not crabbed, not decrepit: lined, marked, used – who are glowing, renewed. Even youth and age can superimpose. The real question for the old actor is whether in an art that so renews him he could also, if he actively wished, find another growth. The question for the audience, happy and refreshed by a joyous evening at the theatre, is also the same one. Is there a further possibility? We know a fleeting liberation can happen; can something also stay?

Here the question comes back to the spectator. Does he want any change in his circumstances? Does he want anything different in himself, his life, his society? If he doesn't, then he doesn't need the theatre to be an acid, a magnifying glass, a searchlight or a place of confrontation.

On the other hand, he may need one or all of these things. In this case, he not only needs the theatre, he needs everything he can get there. He desperately needs that trace that scorches, he desperately needs it to stay.

We are on the verge of a formula, an equation that reads *Theatre* $= R \ r \ a$. To arrive at these letters we are forced to draw from an unexpected source. The French language does not contain the words adequate for the translation of

Shakespeare, yet strangely it is just in this language that we find three words used every day which reflect the problems and the possibilities of the theatre event.

Repetition, representation, assistance, The words work just as well in English. But we normally speak of a rehearsal: *repetition* say the French, and their word conjures up the mechanical side of the process. Week after week, day after day, hour after hour, practice makes perfect. It is a drudge, a grind, a discipline; it is a dull action that leads to a good result. As every athlete knows, repetition eventually brings about change: harnessed to an aim, driven by a will, repetition is creative. There are cabaret singers who practise a new song again and again for a year or more before venturing to perform it in public: then they may repeat this song to audiences for a further fifty years. Laurence Olivier repeats lines of dialogue to himself again and again until he conditions his tongue muscles to a point of absolute obedience – and so gains total freedom. No clown, no acrobat, no dancer would question that repetition is the only way certain actions become possible, and anyone who refuses the challenge of repetition knows that certain regions of expression are automatically barred to him. At the same time, repetition is a word with no glamour. it is a concept without warmth: the immediate association is a deadly one. Repetition is the piano lessons we remember from childhood, the repeated scales; repetition is the touring musical comedy repeating automatically, with its fifteenth cast, actions that have lost their meaning and lost their savour. Repetition is what leads to all that is meaningless in tradition: the soul-destroying long run, the understudy rehearsals, all that sensitive actors dread. These carbon-copy imitations are lifeless. Repetition denies the living. It is as though in one word we see the essential contradiction in the theatre form. To evolve, something needs to be prepared and the preparation often involves going over the same ground again and again. Once completed, this needs to be seen and may evoke a legitimate demand to be repeated again and again. In this repetition, lie the seeds of decay.

What can reconcile this contradiction? Here, the French word for performance – *representation* – contains an answer. A representation is the occasion when something is represented, when something from the past is shown again – something that once was, now is. For representation it is not an imitation or description of a past event, a representation denies time. It abolishes that difference between yesterday and today. It takes yesterday's action and makes it live again in every one of its aspects – including its immediacy. In other words, a representation is what it claims to be – a making present. We can see how this is the renewal of the life that repetition denies and it applies as much to rehearsal as to performance.

The study of what exactly this means opens a rich field. It compels us to see what living action means, what constitutes a real gesture in the immediate present, what forms the fakes assume, what is partially alive, what is completely artificial – until slowly we can begin to define the actual factors that make the act of representation so difficult. And the more we study this the more we see that for a repetition to evolve into a representation, something further is called for. The making present will not happen by itself, help is needed. This help is not always there: yet without this true aid, the true making present will not take place. We wonder what this necessary ingredient could be, and we look at a rehearsal, watching the actors toiling away at their painful repetitions. We realize that in a vacuum their work would be meaningless. Here we find a clue. It leads us naturally to the idea of an audience; we see that without an audience there is no goal, no sense. What is an audience? In the French language amongst the different terms for those who watch, for public, for spectator, one word stands out, is different in quality from the rest. *Assistance* – I watch a play: *j'assiste à une pièce*. To assist – the word is simple: it is the key. An actor prepares, he enters into a process that can turn lifeless at any point. He sets out to capture something, to make it incarnate. In rehearsal, the vital element of assistance comes from the director, who is there to aid by watching. When the actor goes in front of an audience, he finds that the magic transformation does not work by magic. The spectators may just stare at the spectacle, expecting the actor to do all the work and before a passive gaze he may find that all he can offer is a repetition of rehearsals. This may disturb him deeply, he may put all his goodwill, integrity, ardour into working up liveliness and yet he senses all the time a lack. He talks about a 'bad' house. Occasionally, on what he calls a 'good night', he encounters an audience that by chance brings an active interest and life to its watching role – this audience assists. With this assistance, the assistance of eyes and focus and desires and enjoyment and concentration, repetition turns into representation. Then the word representation no longer separates actor and audience, show and public: it envelops them: what is present for one is present for the other. The audience too has undergone a change. It has come from a life outside the theatre that is essentially repetitive to a special arena in which each moment is lived more clearly and more tensely. The audience assists the actor, and at the same time for the audience itself assistance comes back from the stage.

Repetition, representation, assistance. These words sum up the three elements, each of which is needed for the event to come to life. But the essence is still lacking, because any three words are static, any formula is inevitably an attempt to capture a truth for all time. Truth in the theatre is always on the move.

As you read this book, it is already moving out of date. It is for me an exercise, now frozen on the page. But unlike a book, the theatre has one special characteristic. It is always possible to start again. In life this is a myth; we ourselves can never go back on anything. New leaves never turn, clocks never go back, we can never have a second chance. In the theatre the slate is wiped clean all the time.

* * *

In everyday life, 'if' is a fiction, in the theatre 'if' is an experiment.

In everyday life, 'if' is an evasion, in the theatre 'if' is the truth.

When we are persuaded to believe in this truth, then the theatre and life are one.

This is a high aim. It sounds like hard work.

To play needs much work. But when we experience the work as play, then it is not work any more.

A play is play.

PETER BROOK

Peter Brook was born in London and received his M.A. at Oxford, where he founded the Oxford University Film Society. He has been a director of the Royal Shakespeare Company and currently heads the International Centre of Theatre Research in Paris.

He has directed over fifty productions, among them "Love's Labour's Lost," "The Tempest," and "KIng Lear" in Stratford-upon-Avon; "Ring Around the Moon," "Oedipus," "A View from the Bridge," and "Hamlet" in London; "Sergeant Musgrave's Dance," "The Conference of the Birds," "To Moan of Athens," "The Mahabharata," "The Cherry Orchard," and "The Tempest" in Paris; "The Visit," "Marat/Sade," "A Midsummer Night's Dream," and "The Tragedy of Carmen," in New York. His most recent production "The Man Who" began a worldwide tour in 1993.

His films include "Lord of the Flies," "King Lear," and "Meetings with Remarkable Men," among others. His operas include "The Marriage of Figaro," and "Boris Godunov" at Covent Garden and "Faust" and "Eugene Onegin" at the Metropolitan Opera, and most recently, "Impressions de Pelleas".

In addition to THE EMPTY SPACE and THE OPEN DOOR (published in England in 1987 as THE SHIFTING POINT), he has written numerous articles.